Elbridge Smith

The life and character of the Hon. William Parkinson Greene:

An address delivered before the alumni of the Norwich Free Academy, January 25,

1865

Elbridge Smith

The life and character of the Hon. William Parkinson Greene:
An address delivered before the alumni of the Norwich Free Academy, January 25, 1865

ISBN/EAN: 9783337728441

Printed in Europe, USA, Canada, Australia, Japan

Cover: Foto ©ninafisch / pixelio.de

More available books at **www.hansebooks.com**

THE LIFE AND CHARACTER

OF THE

Hon. WILLIAM PARKINSON GREENE.

AN ADDRESS DELIVERED BEFORE THE

ALUMNI OF THE NORWICH FREE ACADEMY,

JANUARY 25, 1865,

BY

ELBRIDGE SMITH, A.M.,

PRINCIPAL OF THE NORWICH FREE ACADEMY.

CAMBRIDGE:
PRINTED AT THE RIVERSIDE PRESS.
1865.

Justum et tenacem propositi virum
Non civium ardor prava jubentium,
   Non vultus instantis tyranni
   Mente quatit solida, neque Auster,
Dux inquieti turbidus Hadriæ,
Nec fulminantis magna manus Jovis;
   Si fractus illabatur orbis,
   Impavidum ferient ruinæ.

                  HORACE, III. 3.

ADDRESS.

ALUMNI OF THE NORWICH FREE ACADEMY:

Ladies and Gentlemen,— We have met this evening to manifest our regard for the memory of one who, for forty years, was one of the most marked and influential men in this community. The motives which have prompted you to this commemorative service do you honor, not only as graduates of the Free Academy, but as citizens, as men and women. Good lives are not so common that we can afford to permit those that are preëminently so to pass from among us without pausing to notice the elements of their excellence and derive from them the lessons which they seem specially designed to impart. The life of every man has been declared to be a plan of God; even Shakspeare has said,—

> "There's a divinity that shapes our ends,
> Rough-hew them how we will."

And a greater than Shakspeare has said, "Ye are God's husbandry, ye are God's building." True lives, it is no exaggeration to say, are divine; they present the lineaments of that divine image in which man was first created; they enlarge our ideas of the capacity of our nature; they stimulate and encourage, they rebuke and warn us. Such were the effects of the life and teachings of Socrates upon the gifted but wayward Alcibiades. "Whenever I heard Pericles or any other great orator," he says in the "Banquet," "I was entertained and delighted; I felt that he had spoken well; but no mortal speech has ever excited in my mind such emotions as are kindled by this magician. When I hear him, I am, as it were, charmed and fettered; my heart leaps like an inspired corybant; my inmost soul is stung by his words as by the bite of a serpent; it is indignant at its own rude and ignoble character. I often weep tears of regret, and think how base and inglorious is the life I lead. Nor am I the only one who weeps like a child and despairs of himself; many others are affected in the same way."

History has been defined to be philosophy teaching by example. But history is made up largely of biography. The lives of communities and States, which are recorded in history, are but the resultants of the lives of the individuals that compose them; and the direction and character of these composite lives which we see in communities, in States, and empires, in the whole course of human history, are determined by comparatively few individuals, who become, as it were, the file-leaders in the great march of human events. What is the secret of that reverential awe which we experience as we enter the sacred shades of Mount Vernon? Is it merely that there are entombed the remains of a statesman and a warrior? Or is it rather the feeling which moved Lord Erskine to write to Washington while living: "I have a large acquaintance among the most valuable and exalted classes of men; but you are the only being for whom I ever felt an awful reverence. I sincerely pray God to grant a long and serene evening to a life so gloriously devoted to the universal happiness of the world." A Chaldean sheik went out from his native country, not knowing whither he went, and became the father of the faithful in all succeeding generations. A single life, of short duration, spent mainly among the hills and valleys of Galilee and ended in ignominy at Calvary, has become the light to lighten the world. But not to multiply examples, how frequently do we find that one true life has moulded the life of the entire community in which it was passed. Who that has witnessed the enthusiasm awakened by the appearance in public of such men as Josiah Quincy and Benjamin Silliman, has not felt how large a portion of their lives has been breathed into the academic and civic life with which they have been associated?

Such is the character of the life which we are this evening met to commemorate, — a life so related to this whole community as to constitute an important element of its history, and so related to you in particular as to command your gratitude and love.

WILLIAM PARKINSON GREENE, the second son of Gardiner* and Elizabeth Hubbard Greene, was born in Boston, the 7th of September, 1795. His father was one of the most eminent merchants of his time, and is still well remembered in Boston as one of the leading financiers and capitalists of the first quarter of this century. He received his elementary education in the schools of Boston, and principally under two teachers whose names have become historic in the State of Mas

* See Appendix, Note A.

sachusetts. These were William Wells and Jacob A. Cummings. Mr. Wells was of English birth, and was for a time connected as a student with the dissenting college at Hackney, for which he was fitted under the instruction of the celebrated Gilbert Wakefield. His father was an intimate friend of the great philosopher, Joseph Priestley, and it was in consequence of the father's attachment to the fortunes of that great man that both father and son removed to this country in 1793. He completed his education at Harvard College, and was for many years one of the most distinguished teachers of Boston. He was also the senior partner and founder of the well-known publishing firm of Wells & Lilly. Mr. Cummings was well known not only as a teacher, but also as an author. His school-books were extensively used in New England, and he also is well remembered as the senior member of the publishing firm of Cummings & Hillard. Under these teachers Mr. Greene was fitted for Harvard College, and entered the Freshman Class in 1810, — the class that enrolls upon its catalogue the names of President James Walker, Dr. F. W. P. Greenwood, the historian Prescott, with whom he was for a time a room-mate, and others who have attained honorable distinction in Church and State. The college life of Mr. Greene was not distinguished for brilliant scholarship, though he gave abundant evidence of possessing decided ability. He was but a boy when he entered college, and he graduated at an age when his collegiate course would more profitably have been commenced. He had not, as yet, begun to take a serious view of life; and, though he was never "vicious or perverse," the playful and sportive elements of his character, which were so prominent in his mature life, were probably the ruling forces of his nature at this period. There were not wanting, however, instances in which his higher powers shone forth with something of that lustre which marked his manhood.

On one occasion, in consequence of his frequent absence from college duties, he was summoned to the room of one of the officers, to receive what is called, at Harvard, a "private," that is, an admonition or warning against further neglect of duty, attended with some loss of rank. On receiving this admonition, which was given by a teacher whom he much respected, he bowed respectfully, and simply remarked, "I have nothing further to say, Sir, than that I shall endeavor to do better in future." From that time to the end of the academic year, he was not absent from a single college exercise. At the expiration of the year he received another summons to appear before the whole faculty. This summons he obeyed with alacrity, concluding that his fidelity was to receive a proper recognition. But what was his surprise, on appearing before that august academic body, to find that he had been summoned to receive a "public," that is, a still stronger censure for neglect of duty, together with the startling announcement that a letter had been sent to his father. This surprise, however, did not throw him from his self-possession, but merely roused him. Calling respectfully upon the President for a statement of his deficiencies, he inquired if there had been any registered against him since he received his first admonition. On examination it was found that there were none since that period. The boy of seventeen then proceeded to express his views upon the subject with a freedom and earnestness quite unusual in the sittings of that body; and those who know the bearing of Mr. Greene when he was thoroughly roused can easily understand that the faculty on that occasion received a much more impressive admonition than they gave. The result was that the letter to his father was recalled.

On another occasion he was sentenced to go over again the studies of an entire term, in consequence of his failure at the regular examination. He presented himself to the gentleman to whom he was sent to make up these deficiencies, and requested, if agreeable, that he might be permitted to recite in one branch each day until the work was completed. His request was granted. At his first interview with his tutor he continued his recitation until the latter, becoming somewhat weary, inquired of him how much he had done. "The whole, Sir," was the reply. The next day he met his teacher again for recitation in another branch, and with the same result. At the close of the first week the entire work of the term was dispatched. He was dismissed by his tutor with a most emphatic "Well done!"

Leaving college at the early age of nineteen, he had made no choice of a profession, nor formed any serious plans for his future life. It was rather in compliance with his father's earnestly expressed desire that he should do something, than from any feeling of choice for the profession, that he decided to begin the study of law. On making this decision he entered the office of his brother-in-law, Samuel Hubbard, Esq., — an office which had acquired the most lucrative practice that had been attained by any law-office in New England up to that time. Charles Jackson, one of the brightest names in the judicial history of the State, had just left this office for a seat on the bench of the Supreme Court, a position to which Mr. Hubbard was also elevated some years later. It was while engaged in the study of his profession that an event occurred which had a marked and probably a decisive influence upon his whole future life. While engaged in an innocent game of chance with several companions, he made use of several profane expressions, which induced one of his friends earnestly but kindly to reprove him. His feelings were at first aroused, and he was tempted to reproach his friend; but, controlling himself, he thanked him, and promised to consider the subject. He did consider it, and came to the conclusion that his friend was right and he was wrong. This incident led him to a careful self-examination, which induced him to retire for several months from the city, and to withdraw himself almost wholly from society. He applied himself, however, closely to his law-books; and on his return to his father's house he found himself, to use his own words, "an altered man." It was about the same time that an older friend, the gentleman for whom he was named, suggested to him that he had talents which might make him a man of influence in the world. This suggestion also had its effect. These incidents of his early youth are of interest, as showing the nice susceptibilities of his nature and his readiness to heed admonition or reproof. His self-respect was a marked feature of his character, but he always felt that he never respected himself so truly as when he corrected his faults or made amends for his errors.

After completing the study of his profession, he became a partner with Mr. Hubbard, and applied himself closely to the performance of its duties. His mind was remarkably well adapted to these labors, and he made rapid progress in the acquisition of professional power. He could not, however, content himself merely with the practice of his profession. To be merely a lawyer, though he were a great lawyer, would by no means satisfy the demands of his nature; he must also be a man; nor could he satisfy himself with anything short of the highest type of manhood.

That we may be able to understand more completely the character which we are considering, it will be necessary to pause for a moment and notice the prevailing influences under which it was formed. It appears to have been a law of the Homeric poetry that the arming of the hero for battle should form a part of the description of the battle itself. In this, as in all other respects, the great father of poetry has only followed a fundamental law of the human mind. We delight to dwell upon every circumstance of splendid preparation which contributes to fit the great man for the scene of his glory. We delight to watch, fold by fold, the bracing on of his Vulcanian panoply, and observe with pleased anxiety the leading forth of that chariot, which, borne on irresistible wheels and drawn by steeds of immortal race, is to crush the necks of the mighty, and sweep away the serried strength of armies. And especially do we delight in this when the conflict is moral and not material. Jesus, inquiring of the doctors of the law in the temple, and Saul of Tarsus, at the feet of Gamaliel, are objects of far greater interest than Achilles girding on his divine armor, or Hannibal at the altar swearing eternal hatred to Rome.

The nascent period of Mr. Greene's life was passed at a time when the entire moral and political life of this nation was in a transition state. The great storm of the French Revolution, which had swept the civilized world for a quarter of a century, had subsided into a calm as remarkable as the convulsion that preceded it. Men were glad, yes, thrice glad, to beat their swords into ploughshares and their spears into pruning-hooks. They were rejoiced to have their attention occupied by something more spiritual than a new revolution in Paris, a new coalition against France, an embargo, or a Hartford convention. Men were tired of hating and slaughtering each other, and, from sheer weariness or desire of change, if from no higher motive, were willing to cultivate the virtues of benevolence and the arts of peace. Hence the great religious and philanthropic enterprises which mark the century sprung at once into lives of intense activity. The city of Boston, always first in the works of benevolence and philanthropy, was the centre of many of these great movements. The American Board of Commissioners for Foreign Missions, which had just been organized, settled there as the home of its organic life. Through its agency the Christian minds of the country were opening for the reception of the great truth of the universal brotherhood of mankind. JEREMIAH

EVARTS, the master-spirit of this and all kindred movements, might often have been seen at the law-office of Messrs. Hubbard & Greene. Mr. Hubbard, at a very early period, took a seat as member of the executive board, and his young partner was naturally drawn to the monthly concerts at Park Street Church, which then attracted so large a portion of the attention of the religious public in Boston. It was at this time that names which now have attained a world-wide celebrity were first awakening admiration by their unselfish and Christian heroism. This was the time when JUDSON and HALL and MILLS and RICE were leading on the sacramental host to a nobler crusade than any that was preached by Peter the Hermit.

The condition of the religious public in Boston during these years was no less a matter of interest. The liberal portion of the congregational churches was beginning to assume a sectarian form, under the guidance of some of the most gifted spirits of the age. The orthodox, or evangelical party, as it was termed, was rousing from the slumbers and formalism of half a century to a higher Christian life and a more enlightened course of Christian action. The collisions of theological opinion were very severe, and the results have doubtless to a great extent been salutary and permanent. It was during these years that ANDREWS NORTON was preparing to reconstruct the evidences of the genuineness of the evangelical records, with a logical compactness and fulness of learning and a rhetorical grace that have seldom been equalled and never surpassed; that the WARES, father and son, were sending forth from the cloister and from the pulpit some of the choicest productions that graced the Christian literature of the first half of this century; that WILLIAM ELLERY CHANNING was passing at the Federal Street Church that pastorate which was to become immortal in American ecclesiastical history; that CHARLES LOWELL was devoting to his ministry at the West Church the fruits of the ripest foreign culture and the virtues of a noble Christian heart.

In the Brattle Street pulpit, still vocal with the eloquence and hallowed by the piety and learning of JOSEPH STEVENS BUCKMINSTER, the mantle of that lamented scholar and divine had fallen upon a young clergyman, not yet turned of his majority, who had come to the sacred office in obedience to the summons of his predecessor; who was but three years the academic senior of Mr. Greene, and had been his tutor in college; whose scholarship surpassed all the traditions of the time, and the fervor of whose appeals drew tears from eyes unused to weep; who early left the service of the altar for a ministry at large, to bear unstained the holy fillets of the priesthood through the perilous paths of statesmanship and diplomacy, — to inspire his own and succeeding generations with the pure enthusiasm of patriotic virtue by embalming the great lessons of our early history in periods of strength and beauty that will be read and recited, like Homeric rhapsodies, while the language we speak retains its meaning in the ears of men, — to plead in our collegiate halls the cause of liberal studies, and in every city and hamlet the cause of the useful arts, — to stand enrobed with the highest honors in the hoary cloisters and storied halls of Oxford and Cambridge, yet gain far greater honors as the patron of the American common school,*— to win easy triumphs over the trained diplomatists of Europe, and adapt the highest truths of science to the comprehension of the common day-laborer,— to be the mediator of a new covenant between all that is beautiful, useful, and true in the literatures, arts, and civilizations of the Old World and the manly virtues and free principles that were springing into life in the New,— to make our highways and by-ways of barbarous name as honored as the Appian and sacred ways of Roman renown,— and to teach the uncouth vocabularies of our Puritan and American dialects to move in the grand processions of his sentences with the grace of Apollos and the beauty of Hyperions; whose later years were spent in a noble but vain endeavor to bind the hearts of his countrymen in indissoluble bonds of affection and gratitude to the nation's shrine at Mount Vernon, and, when all the ministries of peace had failed to heal the maladies of the times, and the mad demon of war was let loose in the land, to summon his countrymen to arms with an eloquence no less classic and far more successful than that which

> "Shook the arsenal and fulmined over Greece
> To Macedon and Artaxerxes' throne;"

whose last public appeal, in behalf of returning prodigals, beneath the arches of Faneuil Hall, which had so often echoed back the plaudits of his rapt and crowded auditories, was in touching harmony with the

---

* The acts establishing the Massachusetts Board of Education and the State Normal Schools bear the official signature of Edward Everett, as the executive of the State.

last utterances at Calvary; whose death the last week shook the very pillars of the State; and around whose bier, as he was borne so tenderly to the peaceful shades of our modern Ceramicus, his partisan foes of every name thronged, to mingle their tears and swell the chorus of praise which admiring friends had always accorded to the exalted talents, the varied attainments, and the Christian virtues of EDWARD EVERETT.

It was during these years also that FRANCIS WAYLAND, at the First Baptist Church, by a single effort, placed himself in the front rank of American moralists and thinkers, and gave the first fitting expressions to the religious and patriotic spirit of the age, in his sermons on "The Moral Dignity of the Missionary Enterprise," and "The Duties of an American Citizen"; that BENJAMIN B. WISNER was maintaining at the Old South Church, with singular ability and energy, the faith of the fathers, and breathing into the old ecclesiastical forms and formularies the breath of a new spiritual life. And last, but not least, it was during these years that the clarion voice of LYMAN BEECHER began to be heard in Boston; and among the crowds that gathered to the Park Street Church * to hang upon the lips of this son of thunder might frequently have been seen the young lawyer whose life and character we are considering.

Such were some of the salient features and prominent actors in the religious public at the period when Mr. Greene was entering upon his professional life. In civil life, and in the circle of his own profession, there were scenes and actors of equal interest. The Suffolk bar

---

* The period referred to was previous to Dr. Beecher's settlement in Hanover Street, which did not occur until 1826.

at that time, as always, comprised a galaxy of learning and talent second to that of no other bar in the country. There might still have been seen in court practitioners who had tried their first cases as loyal subjects of King George III.; and there were still conspicuous the stately bearing, the courteous dignity, and the professional self-respect, which, under the Colonial rule, had been derived from the practice and usages of lord high chancellors and chief justices of the Court of King's Bench. JOHN ADAMS was still living, like Homer's Nestor to remind the rising generation of the eventful struggles that ushered in the dawn of our national life; while his distinguished son was astonishing the diplomatic circles of Europe by the extent of his erudition, or, as first minister of the cabinet at Washington, proving himself master of the highest duties of State. WILLIAM PRESCOTT, the father of the historian, was holding by general consent the first place in the Massachusetts bar. HARRISON GRAY OTIS, just passing the prime of his manly beauty, still reminded the bar and the forum of that eloquence by which his distinguished relative had struck the key-note of the Revolution. JOSIAH QUINCY, now in the high noon of his noble manhood, had just closed his stormy but brilliant congressional career, and was directing the ample resources of his mind to the principles of municipal law, and laying the foundations of the present prosperity and civil order of his native city. At that time, too, occurred an event which produced some commotion in the Suffolk bar, which felt quite competent to transact the legal business of Boston without the aid of imported talent. In passing down Court Street in the year 1816, there might have been seen the sign of a new claimant for legal patronage, "DANIEL WEBSTER, Attorney and Counsellor at Law." This new candidate for public favor, in the language of one of the profession, had "come from the backwoods," and was hardly yet well versed in the habits and customs of good society. He managed, however, to get on tolerably well, and is now better known to the world than when he first stirred the jealousy of the elder, and roused the ambition of the younger members of the Boston bar.

Nor should I forget to notice the new direction that Boston capital had already begun to take under the restrictions that the Embargo had imposed upon foreign commerce, and the stimulus it had given to domestic manufactures. While William P. Greene was studying his classics and mathematics in the cloisters of Harvard College, FRANCIS C. LOWELL and PATRICK T. JACKSON, at the distance of only a few miles, in Waltham, were bending their thoughts to the re-invention of the machine that was to revolutionize New-England life, and emancipate our Yankee girls from the slavery of the hand-loom and spinning-wheel, and send them to the school-room and the seminary. While Mr. Greene was making his way through his Blackstone and Coke upon Littleton, Francis C. Lowell was far away in Washington, instilling into the mind of JOHN C. CALHOUN, not yet poisoned by the heresies of nullification and secession, the principles of the protective system. What beginnings of woes and blessings here pass under our notice! From this friendly interview between these sons of Massachusetts and South Carolina, (the positive and negative poles of our whole social and political system,) there sprung, under the lead of Mr. Calhoun, a course of legislation which was made a pretext for nullification in 1832, and, with a change of issues, for secession in 1860. The present results to the South from the erratic conduct and disorganizing principles of the great nullifier, we see in desolated fields, in prostrate commerce, and smouldering ruins, from the Potomac to the Rio Grande. In the North there has sprung into existence, under the same legislation, and in spite of all its fluctuations, an industrial life which has carried the star of our empire westward to the Pacific, and summoned to its aid every grade of talent and skill from the bogs of Ireland and the workshops of England and Germany.

In commercial and financial circles there were names that have attained a national renown. The firm of A. & A. LAWRENCE, by whose talent, enterprise, and well-earned profits, treaties were to be made, cabinets moulded, cities founded, colleges and academies endowed, charities and asylums established for the relief of every ill that flesh or spirit is heir to, was formed the same year that Mr. Greene was graduated from college. The APPLETONS, SAMUEL, NATHAN, and WILLIAM, a noble triumvirate of benevolence, integrity, and mercantile wisdom; THOMAS HANDASYD PERKINS, "whose heart was as much larger than his fortune as his fortune was larger than a beggar's"; JAMES LLOYD, respected alike for his ability and success in commercial life, and for his address and talent as a member of the United States Senate; and, in the purely financial department of commerce, the honored father of our lamented friend, GARDINER GREENE, whose skill and integrity were recognized in his appointment to the presidency of the Boston branch of the United States Bank;—these are a few of the more prominent names representing the men who in the Boston of forty years ago laid the foundations of what we see in the Boston of to-day; who raised commerce far above the selfish pursuit of private gain, and taught their own and succeeding generations that it is a great calling of humanity, having high duties and generous aims,—one of the noblest developments of our modern civilization.

The political world at this period was in a state of unusual ferment. The contest between the Federalists and Democrats was far more bitter, though less bloody, than it has been even in our own times. The streets of Boston were the scenes of personal and even of murderous conflict. The partisan warfare carried on in their respective journals by BENJAMIN RUSSELL and BENJAMIN AUSTIN will always form a marked chapter in the history of American journalism. The bitterness of these political contests stimulated intellectual action, and by its very excesses awakened a desire for higher and calmer discussions of the great questions of state and literature than mere partisan journals could permit. This desire found expression in the establishment of the "North American Review."

The close of the war with Great Britain, and the banishment of Napoleon, were followed by an "era of good feelings" as remarkable as had been the intensity of the previous partisan strife. The force of passion "could no farther go." During the period of calm which followed, some of the older political combatants seemed inclined to retire from the field, and, like wearied Titans, to give up the strife from mere exhaustion. Parties could no longer be marshalled under the old issues. The progress of events had removed the old questions from the field of debate. The times required a new division of party lines, and were favorable for the presentation of new political aspirants. The claims of Mr. Greene were not overlooked. It was felt that he could present an array of influence, social, pecuniary, and political, which would secure for him a rapid advancement and undoubted success. He was accordingly invited to present himself as a candidate for the first grades of political preferment on our modern Athenian *bema* in Faneuil Hall. The offer was carefully considered and deliberately declined. He deemed the moral sacrifices too great. The peril to his integrity far outweighed the promise to his fame. To this decision he adhered through life, with the exception, that, for a single year, he filled very acceptably the office of Mayor of this city.

Such were some of the influences under which Mr. Greene pursued the studies preparatory to his profession, and commenced its practice. At no period of its history, probably, has Boston possessed, in proportion to its population, a greater amount of really useful and active talent, or exhibited in professional, mercantile, and social life, fairer examples of high honor and true manhood, than in the second decade of the present century. And it will be somewhat surprising to one who has given no thought to the subject to observe how large a portion of the influences which now shape New-England society date their origin, or received their permanent impress from this period. These events, and others which have now become some of the landmarks of history, — these actors, whose lives gave so much of their importance to these events,— were in themselves a school of influence and a source of power which ripened into large and generous growth qualities that had only germinated under the formal discipline of the academic and professional curricula. Especially was this the case with a nature so susceptible and capacious as Mr. Greene's. The bare perception of great qualities of character awakened in him a sense of obligation not only to imitate, but to appropriate them, not merely to *ape*, but to *own* them. Accordingly, the manly and heroic virtues sprung up in his early manhood, not as exotics, but as the native products of the soul; and he rose superior to all the allurements of ease and the seductions of pleasure, resolved to bear an honorable part in the battle of life, and to win its laurels, or at least to deserve them.

On the 14th of July, 1819, Mr. Greene was united in marriage to Augusta Elizabeth, daughter of Louis Vassail Borland, a lady of rare accomplishments and most winning manners, a lady whose virtues were at once the solace and the admiration of her husband.

The circumstances under which Mr. Greene passed the brief term of his professional life were not favorable for his acquiring the reputation as a lawyer to which his ability entitled him. As junior member of the firm, the work of the office, rather than the pleadings and arguments in court, devolved upon him.

There are not wanting incidents,[1] however, to show that he was destined to occupy a commanding position at the American bar had circumstances permitted him to continue in his profession. He possessed in an eminent degree all those mental qualities which lie at

[1] The following incidents may serve to illustrate the moral temper with which Mr. Greene commenced the practice of his profession.

A man making high professions of sanctity of character, and of ample means, entered his office on one occasion, and placed in his hands a claim against a laboring man which he wished prosecuted to the full extent of the law, (the laws enforcing imprisonment for debt were, at that time, in full force). Mr. Greene took the claim, and at once commenced the preparation of the necessary papers, and while thus engaged, entered into conversation with his client respecting the moral aspects of the case. "Is not this man honest whom you are about to commit to prison?" said the young lawyer. "He is so far as I know," replied the client. "Is he not industrious?" "I know nothing to the contrary." "Has he not a family dependent upon him?" "I believe he has." "Why, then, do you propose to distress him?" "Because I want my money," was the reply. The conversation proceeded in this strain until the papers were completed, when Mr. Greene, gathering them in his hand, and looking his client earnestly and imploringly in the face, made a final appeal. "I beg you, Sir, not to distress this poor man in this manner." "I don't care; I want my money," was the unfeeling reply. Mr. Greene looked at him in silence for a moment, while his indignation rose to the point of action; then, taking from his pocket the amount of money necessary to pay the debt, he placed it, in connection with the papers, in the hands of his client, and "kicked him down-stairs," with very explicit directions never to enter his office again.

A case of some importance had been intrusted to him, and in the preparation for the trial, Mr. Greene had urged the importance of the strictest veracity in all statements respecting the points at issue. But in the course of the trial it became apparent from the testimony of the opposing party that his client had knowingly deceived him. As soon as he ascertained this, he rose in the bar, and, fixing a withering look upon his client, said to him, "You have lied to me, Sir"; then turning to the court, he said, "May it please your Honor, I have not the case before you that has been represented to me, and I shall prosecute it no further."

These anecdotes may not accord with the precepts of Lord Chesterfield; but if they are deficient in the *suaviter in modo*, they certainly do not lack the *fortiter in re*.

the foundation of great success. A remarkably retentive memory, a quickness of perception, a breadth of comprehension, and a keenness of penetration seldom equalled, were united with a degree of courage and force of will which quailed at no dangers, and yielded to no obstacles. Although he never appeared in Norwich as a lawyer, I have the best authority for saying that his opinions upon difficult points of law were always held in the highest respect; and in the numerous legal questions arising out of a most extensive and complicated business life, in which he had occasion to call to his aid the best legal talent, his own judgment was seldom improved by that of his counsel, or overruled by the decisions of the bench. His career as a lawyer, however, was destined to be of short duration. His father had so far sympathized with the great movement for the establishment of domestic manufactures as to invest considerable sums in these enterprises, and among others the Thames Company at Norwich Falls went into operation in 1823, upon the basis of capital which was furnished by him and other Boston capitalists. The first operations of the company were conducted by the late William C. Gilman, so long and so favorably known in this community. Soon after the company commenced operations, Mr. Gardiner Greene gave to his son the whole amount which he had invested in this city, with the added condition that he should remove hither and take the property under his personal charge. There was also another reason which had a controlling influence in inducing him to remove from Boston to Norwich. His health, which was never really robust, had exhibited alarming symptoms of decline. An attack of hemorrhage had settled the fact that a longer continuance in the law-office would in all probability soon prove fatal. The wish of the father alone was law for the son. He accordingly bade adieu to the home of his youth and to the brilliant prospects that were opening before him in his profession, for the less inviting scenes of a cotton-mill. He left the court-room which had resounded with the eloquence of John Adams and James Otis, and which could promise no honors to which he might not worthily aspire, for the music of the power-loom and the spinning-jenny. The change involved undoubtedly a considerable sacrifice of feeling, and was hardly in accordance with the dictates of his own deliberate judgment. He left the profession in which he was rapidly becoming proficient, for a business of which he had the first principles and all the details to learn. The greatness of the change he did not himself fully realize until the experience of years had taught him that the manufacture of cotton, like the practice of law, was a complicated and even a profound science, and that the ruin of one fortune was necessary to furnish the experience requisite for the accumulation of another.

It was in the summer of 1824 that Mr. Greene removed to this city, and entered upon the new course of life to which circumstances rather than choice had called him. It is even doubtful whether, at the time of his removal, his purpose was fixed to remain here. Whatever may have been his intention, there were elements in his character which forbade him to abandon an enterprise or leave a community in which he had once become interested. We find, accordingly, that he had scarcely become settled in this city before he was a leader in every enterprise connected with its welfare. Within a year after his arrival, he was at the head of the movement which resulted in the organization of the Thames Bank, of which he was made the first President, and over the fortunes of which he continued to preside for the following sixteen years. In 1826 and 1827, he, in connection with Mr. Gilman and several others, was directing his attention to the importance of improving the educational advantages in this community. The extensive but unimproved water-power upon the Shetucket River had already attracted attention, but no systematic efforts had been made for bringing it under the control of human industry. Mr. Greene was the first and largest contributor to the fund for making the survey of the river and determining all the questions preliminary to rendering it available for industrious purposes. Nor do many years elapse before we find the same active and determined spirit thoroughly awake to the importance of increased accommodations for travel and transportation between this city and the great centres of commerce in Boston and New York.

But these events must be considered more in detail; and, in doing so, it will be convenient to divide his life in Norwich into two periods,— the first extending from the time of his settlement here in 1824 to the great financial crisis in 1837; and the second extending from the last-named period until his death. The first of these periods was one of intense and ceaseless activity; and, as I have already intimated, his labors extended to every variety of human interest and to every department of human action. The second was a period of less external activity, but of greater prosperity. During this period he was permitted to realize some of the advantages naturally arising from his previous years of toil, self-sacrifice, and calamity.

In 1825, the traveller through Norwich would have found on the site of the present village of GREENEVILLE [1] — with its population of three thousand souls, and its manufacturing capital of upwards of a million of dollars, with its churches and schools — but a single farmhouse, while the stream that waters it was of little value to the inhabitants, save that in spring-time it afforded them an abundant supply of shad. In his first plan for bridling the Shetucket and compelling it to labor in the service of man, Mr. Greene had in view the manufacture of iron, and relied upon the active cooperation of a man who had large means at his disposal, as well as long experience in this department of mechanical industry. Relying upon his good faith, he had nearly completed his contracts for the necessary extent of land bordering upon the river, when his coadjutor was induced to abandon the Norwich scheme for what appeared a more lucrative field of action in Chelmsford, Mass. Thus forsaken by the gentleman, or I should rather say by the man, whose aid seemed of vital importance to success, he nevertheless persisted in his enterprise, though in a modified form. Abandoning the particular kind of manufacture which he had first proposed, he now directed his attention simply to the purpose of making the great water-power

[1] See Appendix, Note B.

serviceable for any form of industrial service that might be desired. Hence originated the Norwich Water-power Company, which still exists under its original charter.

This company commenced operations on the Shetucket in the spring of 1829, and the work was completed in the following year. In the early part of 1832, the Thames Company laid the foundations of the first cotton-mill in that village, and on its completion hired a large portion of the water-power which had been made available. The operations of the Thames Company had now become quite extended, comprising the cotton and iron manufactures at the Falls, the cotton-mill at Bozrahville, and what was then called the Quinebaug Mill on the Shetucket. The original capital was three hundred thousand dollars, and this was increased in 1825 to five hundred thousand dollars, and at a subsequent period it was still further augmented. The business of the company, however, was never eminently profitable, and in 1837 it shared the fate of a large proportion of similar establishments in the country. Its interests became somewhat involved in those of another manufacturing company, the Norwich and New York Manufacturing Company; and this company, on the failure of the Thames, became the purchaser of the greater portion of its property. The career of the Norwich and New York Company was of short duration; and in October, 1843, its property passed into the hands of the present FALLS COMPANY,[1] which was organized upon the joint-stock prin-

[1] See Appendix, Note C.

ciple, and continues to prosper under that organization until the present time.

It might seem that the water-power and manufacturing companies already mentioned, with all the complications and perplexities incident to their first organization, would have been sufficient to exhaust the energies of a single mind, however active, for a period of ten years. But it was otherwise. The people of Norwich, as early as 1830, began to agitate the subject of constructing a railroad between this city and Worcester, and thus establishing a readier communication with the commercial capital of the New England States. It was natural than an enterprise of this nature, the object of which was to bring his native city into closer communication with the city of his adoption, should warmly enlist his sympathies and thoroughly arouse his energies. It will be remembered, that, through Mr. Greene, Boston capital had already begun to flow pretty freely into Norwich for investment. This circumstance contributed not a little to the success of the undertaking. But the intrinsic magnitude of the work was by no means the only obstacle to be overcome.[1] It required the harmonious and favorable action of the legislatures of two different States. It encountered serious opposition from the rival roads which had been projected on other routes. The peculiar qualities of Mr. Greene's character, his business connections and personal acquaintances in Boston, no less than his large influence here, made him one of the most efficient agents in planning and executing this Herculean task. The younger portion of the population of Norwich, who

[1] See Appendix, Note D.

have not heard, from the actors in this great work or their contemporaries, the greatness of the difficulties attending it, can form but an imperfect idea of their magnitude. It involved the ruin of many a fair fortune in this city, and for a time seemed to threaten the financial destruction of the place. It will be remembered, also, that in the midst of the work the great revulsion of 1837 added greatly to the already gigantic obstacles to be overcome. Through all these years of toil and disaster, Mr. Greene bore more than his individual share of the burdens which the work necessarily laid upon all its friends. At the organization of the company he was one of the largest subscribers to its stock, was one of the original board of directors, was chosen to its presidency, which he declined to accept, and it was by his personal influence at one of the most critical junctures of the road, that the credit of the State of Massachusets was finally obtained, and the success of the project placed beyond a doubt.

The commencement of operations upon the road in the spring of 1836 was signalized by a grand civil and military display, marking as it did an era in the commercial and industrial history of the city. On that occasion, a stranger might have seen among the worthies of the day a man of slight frame and pallid countenance, an invalid, to all appearance, who had just received his discharge from his sick chamber, and had come out to seek in the excitement and joyousness of the occasion a restoration of his wasted strength. An intelligent resident would have informed him that in that quiet and unassuming person was found the real genius and ruling spirit of the enterprise ; that it was to his convincing logic and resolute will that legislative bodies and council boards were to yield a cordial assent; that at his command the coffers of the Old Bay State — never closed when any great or good cause is in need of aid — would be cheerfully opened ; that by his unbending integrity and determined courage fraud would be exposed and rebuked, and the whole work at last triumphantly completed.

I have repeatedly referred to the financial crisis in 1837 as an important era in Mr. Greene's life. It was at this time that he saw the princely fortune which he had inherited from his father entirely swept away. He was not, however, reduced to absolute bankruptcy. "I did suppose," he once remarked, " in 1837, that I was worth something, but it subsequently appeared that I was worth nothing ; that on which I had relied as possessing some value proved to be utterly worthless." But the ruin of his fortune had brought no stain upon his character. That fortune had not been wasted in the pursuit of pleasure ; it had not been made the sport of any sordid or selfish ambition. It had disappeared in the varying fortunes of business, and had been honestly invested in enterprises that promised not only a profit to the owner, but lasting benefits to this and other communities. But if he had not grown rich, he certainly had become wise. What he had lost in material property he had more than gained in that wealth of character which no vicissitudes could destroy.

In readjusting his shattered fortunes, it became necessary to seek for a time some pecuniary aid. His first applications were not successful. In this emergency his brother, Benjamin D. Greene,[1] from whom he had neither asked nor intended to ask any aid, met him, while he was on a visit to Boston, and quietly placed in his hand a small slip of paper. On examination he found it to be a check for twenty thousand dollars. Surprised by this unexpected act of fraternal confidence and affection, he handed it back with the familiar remark, "I shall not take this, Ben." "I shall not be pleased if you do not, Will, after mortgaging my house to get it for you." He did accept the offered favor, and remarked, a few years since, in relating the circumstance, "It is some satisfaction to me to know that my brother is worth fifty thousand dollars more to-day than he would have been had he not loaned me that money." And here I cannot but remark that the foregoing incident was only a representative act of the relations that existed between these brothers. Throughout their entire lives they cherished the most confiding fraternal affection, without one unkind act or word, while the services and the fortunes of each were always at the disposal of the other, as the varying fortunes of life might demand. Surely we may say, "Behold, how good and how pleasant it is for brethren to dwell together in unity!" And it is but proper to add, as the fortune of the elder brother was largely invested in this city, in the various enterprises directed by the younger, that he shared largely, perhaps equally in those mental and moral qualities which so long and so extensively blessed this community. He received his elementary education in the Edinburgh

---

[1] See Appendix, Note E.

High School, was graduated at Harvard College, attained high distinction as a man of science, possessing, at the time of his death, the best private herbarium in the country. This great botanical collection, together with an additional legacy of ten thousand dollars, and his valuable library, was given to the "Boston Society of Natural History," in which he always took a deep interest and of which he was the first president.

The whole attention of Mr. Greene, during the first period of his Norwich life, was not absorbed in developing the natural resources and advancing the material welfare of the city. I have already noticed his early attempts to improve the educational advantages in this community. He was none the less mindful of its religious interests. At an early period in the history of the Thames Company, provision was made for the spiritual wants of the operatives by the erection of a small chapel, which for years he made his regular place of worship. At this time he was not only the temporal but the spiritual adviser of those who were engaged in the mills under his direction. The majority of his operatives were protestants, and the great barrier which now divides the religious sympathies of employers and employees did not at that time exist. The chapel of which I have spoken soon became too small to meet the demand that was made upon it, and increased accommodations were obtained by the erection of the tasteful edifice now occupied by the Methodists, on Sachem Street. The principal part of the expense of erecting this church was eventually paid by Mr. Greene out of his own pocket.

The history of this portion of Mr. Greene's life

merits a much more extended and minute narrative than I have given it. It is a matter of great regret that he has left us no record of these events, so important to the historian of this city, beyond plain business transactions and official records, important portions of which have already been consumed by fire. He was quite indifferent even to the honest fame to which his enterprise and achievements entitled him; and he has left no diary or other personal writings from which we can gather the internal history of the man. Success in laudable endeavors was to him a sufficient reward, and failure he encountered not with mere stoical indifference, but with Christian heroism.

The second portion of Mr. Greene's life we may date from the organization of the SHETUCKET COMPANY in 1838. This company was formed in part from the ruins of the Thames Company, by the purchase of the Quinebaug Mill at Greeneville, by William P. and Benjamin D. Greene and Samuel Mowry. The Falls Company was organized in October, 1843, and these two companies, in the improved circumstances of the country and in the increased wisdom of those who directed their affairs, at once entered upon a career of prosperity. The losses of previous years were in a great measure repaired, and, with one exception, this period of prosperity continued until the close of Mr. Greene's life. In May, 1842, he had the misfortune to see the mill of the Shetucket Company burned to the ground. It was a severe blow both to his fortune and his spirit; but while the smoke was yet rising from the ruins of the first mill, his purpose was formed and steps were taken for the erection of a second. This was speedily completed, and, with some additions, is the large cotton-mill now standing in Greeneville. In 1845 and 1846 his activity was very much restricted by protracted sickness. For nearly two years he was scarcely able to leave his house; still his mind toiled on. During this confinement he went through an elaborate course of experiments, involving all the principles of hydrostatics and hydraulics, and their application to water-wheels and the various forms of engineering involved in their structure and management.

We may pass over the succeeding years of Mr. Greene's history as presenting nothing out of his usual routine of business life and active usefulness, until we reach a period in which we, as friends of the Free Academy, are especially interested. The people of Norwich had been slow to act in sympathy with the great movement which was giving to the State and to the country an improved class of public schools. They came late to the work, and compensated the tardiness of their action by their energy and efficiency when fairly enlisted in the movement. In 1853 a privately printed circular was addressed to the leading business men of this city, by the Rev. John P. Gulliver, soliciting their joint action and pecuniary contributions for the establishment of a literary institution of high order, at an estimated expense of seventy-five thousand dollars. The plan contemplated ten equal subscriptions of the amount of seven thousand five hundred dollars. Mr. Greene was the third individual to whom this circular was submitted. He promptly replied that he would give one tenth of seventy-five thousand dollars, or of any other sum that might be thought necessary for the accomplishment of the object. After securing the amount first proposed, and before the plans for the building were completed, an additional sum of ten thousand dollars was found necessary, and of this additional sum he contributed fifteen hundred dollars. With this subscription the Norwich Free Academy was erected in 1855–6, and dedicated on the 21st of October, 1856. In February, 1857, he contributed the additional sum of one thousand dollars, (as part of a new subscription of five thousand dollars,) to aid in removing some obligations that had been incurred in the erection and furnishing of the building. On the death of Mr. Russell Hubbard, in June, 1857, who had been elected first President of the Corporation and Board of Trustees, Mr. Greene was chosen to succeed him; and he was continued in that office by successive elections until his death. During these seven years he not only held the office, but filled it. From the commencement of the enterprise he had done much towards moulding its character, and some of its most important features are due to his influence. Mr. Hubbard, his predecessor in office, used often to speak of him as "*his right-hand man.*" It was his official and individual aim not only to render the academy a first-class school in every department usually included in a high-school course of instruction, but to place its advantages on equal terms for all the inhabitants of Norwich. If he discriminated at all, that discrimination was shown in favor of the less affluent portion of the community. His labors and his benefactions, in connection with this institution, were emphatically works of love. Whenever any business connected with the Free Academy required his attention, he was always ready. In my official intercourse of seven years with him, I was never denied a hearing in consequence of some other engagement, nor on account of the infirm state of his health, which often confined him to his chamber; and, more than this, I always found him cheerful. If there had been losses incurred, if mistakes had been made, if disasters had befallen us, instead of manifesting any impatience, he would receive the announcement with a cheerful smile, and oftentimes with an exhibition of his inimitable pleasantry. I never asked him for a farthing for the Academy, and yet he expended through me more than fifteen hundred dollars* in various ways, which he never reported to the treasurer. When questions of importance arose, it was wonderful to witness his capacity for labor and his willingness to perform it; and that, too, when others felt that he was entitled to exemption. In all investigations affecting character he was remarkable alike for his courage and his painstaking efforts to get at the exact truth. How little does this community know of the toils through which he passed in connection with some cases of difficulty that came before him; and it was all done without a murmur and without a censure! He had a great partiality for hearing both sides of a question, and in fact did not consider himself qualified to decide a case justly until both sides of it had been carefully examined. He was one of the best school legislators I ever knew; and this was the more surprising from the fact that his entire life had been spent in the consideration of great interests and in business pursuits

* See Appendix, Note F.

which had no connection with the internal policy of the school-room. The playfulness of his nature was often exhibited in connection with his acts of generosity; and it seems to me but proper to relate some of these, as they may give to those who have never known him a more distinct impression of his character. At the dedication of the Free Academy a valuable pianoforte had been borrowed to furnish the necessary accompaniment in the musical entertainment, with the hope that means might in some way be obtained to purchase it for the institution. But months passed away and the piano remained in the school-room unpaid for, and with no person to acknowledge responsibility for its value, nor even for its rent. The owner very naturally desired that some disposition should be made of it. Returning home on the evening of the 29th of April, 1857, I found the following note: —

Mr. Smith:

Dear Sir, — I have this day received payment in full for the pianoforte, stool, and spread, now in the Academy, from the hand of Mr. Levi Muggins.

Yours truly, Geo. H. Martin.

This note produced quite a sensation in our academic circle. The worthy president thought that the piano had been sold to some stranger. The family of "Muggins" was not well known in Norwich; indeed, it was not known at all. Others thought the whole matter a joke. Mr. Martin was evidently in league with Mr. Muggins, as he refused to throw any light on the subject beyond what was contained in his note. The treasurer of the Academy met Mr. Greene at the bank, and accused him of the whole transaction; and after some days of good-natured banter and not unpleasant mystery, the community settled into the conviction that Mr. Levi Muggins was the *nom de plume* of a well-known gentleman on Washington Street, whose fondness for sport and innocent practical jokes was often exhibited in his deeds of charity and benevolence.

In the autumn of the same year, in the darkest period of that terrible financial revulsion, knowing that there were some funds at the disposal of the trustees which had been raised for general purposes, I called on Mr. Greene with reference to purchasing a pair of globes for the use of the school. He inquired of me what size of globes I wanted. I told him I had always thought of thirty-six-inch globes, but that those were no times for such educational luxuries; that eighteen-inch globes would answer very well, if indeed it were advisable to purchase globes of any size. "Get the best terms you can for thirty-six-inch globes," he replied, "and bring them to me. Do you want anything more?" "No," I replied. "Then go," he said, pleasantly; "I must be excused, for I am going to Boston to-night." We shall soon learn what was his business in Boston. When I brought him the price of the globes, he gave me his check for the amount, (one hundred and fifty dollars,) remarking, "Take that for Christmas; I always mean to remember the Free Academy at that time." I afterwards learned, that, on that very day, cheerful and playful as he seemed, there was a weight upon him that would have borne a royal merchant down. At that very time, in addition to the great responsibilities connected with the companies under his charge, he was pledging half his fortune to place the solvency of his friends beyond a doubt. And yet in that period of distress, when the financial foundations of the world seemed out of place, when fortunes of colossal magnitude were dissipated like the mists of the dawn, and men who woke in the morning with the wealth of Crœsus, retired at night only to lodgings provided by charity, he trod the path of his daily duties with as manly a courage and as cheerful a serenity as the mariner walks his quarter-deck while his sails are filled by the most prosperous breezes. I have thought that these particulars, trifling though they may seem, relating to two of the most prominent and useful objects in our school-room, would not, if remembered, mar in the least the music that accompanies our morning devotions, or retard the progress of grateful pupils as they thread their way through all the problems of terrestrial latitude and longitude, or trace the boundaries of Lyra and Andromeda, of Orion and Pleiades, and mount to all the mysteries and harmonies of the galaxies and nebulæ of the highest heavens.

There had been a tacit understanding between Mr. Russell Hubbard and Mr. Greene, and I believe also some other donors to the funds of the Free Academy, that when the institution was fairly started there should be a further addition to its funds. The death of Mr. Hubbard prevented his taking any part in this work, to which he was looking forward with so much pleasure. The object, however, was not lost sight of by Mr. Greene. He partially accomplished this purpose in the second year of his administration, when he united with several others in raising seven thousand five hundred dollars for the Academy; and on the first of January, 1863, he placed in the hands of Mr. Learned, the treasurer, the sum of ten thousand dollars, in the form of seven-thirty bonds, with the understanding that the amount should be increased to fifteen thousand dollars by other friends of the institution. The total amount of his contributions to the Free Academy was little short of thirty thousand dollars. It is proper to notice in this connection, that, on the 7th of September, 1859, Mrs. Augusta E. Greene* saw fit to celebrate her husband's birthday, which also coincided with the birthday of the city, on its bicentennial return, and gave a fitting charm to the festivities of our jubilee by putting into the hands of the treasurer of the Free Academy a deed of the estate now occupied by the Principal, which she had purchased at an expense of seven thousand dollars. And if to this be added the donation of another member of the family, our honored Mayor, the total sum of the contributions from this family falls but little short of forty thousand dollars, — a full third of the entire property of the institution. The princely donations of Mr. Greene, as you well know, were not the only, perhaps not the most important, services rendered by him to the Academy. His labors as a trustee and as the presiding officer will long be remembered by those who were associated with him on the board, as well as by the community at large. The state of his health did not permit him to visit the school, to inspect in person its operations and form that acquaintance with the teachers and scholars that he desired. He excused himself, however, from these duties only on the ground

* See Appendix, Note G.

of necessity. It was to him a matter of self-denial, and he submitted to the privation as to an affliction. His last appearance at any of the exercises of the school was on the occasion of the annual exhibition in 1860. At the close he made some remarks to the pupils in reply to a token of affection which was handed him by the graduating class. It is a matter of regret that an exact report of these remarks has not been preserved. He could not have spoken more appropriately had he known that it was to be his last utterance to the school. "Scholars at your age," he said, "are often inclined to insist upon their rights, and that too, perhaps, when they have not been violated. Let me advise you to be more solicitous to learn your duties than your rights. Seek first to know what you ought to do, and you may expect, as a matter of course, that your rights will be respected. If we take proper care of our duties, our rights will take care of themselves."

I have already observed that the health of Mr. Greene gave early indications of infirmity. From boyhood he had been the victim of a pulmonary complaint, which twenty years ago threatened an immediate termination of his life. In addition to this he suffered seriously from two very severe falls, which, according to all known physical laws, should have proved fatal. It was under these great physical disadvantages that the immense labors of his life were performed. More than fifteen years before his death, a council of physicians pronounced his recovery hopeless, and admitted their inability to render him any further aid. This announcement, which would in the case of most men only have hastened dissolution, merely stirred his energies to encounter his infirmities with his own resolute and determined spirit. He became, for a time, almost exclusively his own physician. He rose superior to all his maladies, and by wisely husbanding his strength, and carefully studying his constitution, he was able still to put forth the energies of his great mind in the successful management of his extensive business. This is by no means the least remarkable feature of his character, that, while suffering from infirmities that, with the great majority of men, would have made them only burdens upon the patience of their friends, he still continued to dispense his wise and powerful influence as a leading mind in the community. Still, for the last twenty years of his life, he was, as it were, under bonds for good behavior; was obliged to regulate his diet, to guard against exposure, and to exercise constantly a degree of circumspection as far beyond the power as it is above the disposition of ordinary men. It was by this despotic control to which in the exercise of his moral and intellectual powers he subjected his physical nature, that he was enabled to prolong his life to the honored verge of threescore years and ten. He was able, by reason of his superior courage, at all times to look his symptoms calmly in the face. There were times long before his death when he thought his end was near, but this conviction produced no discomposure. He walked thoughtfully, but serenely,

> "the silent, solemn shore
> Of that vast ocean he must sail so soon,"

as he thought, and discussed every question pertaining

to his change with the same calmness that he would have arranged the preparations for a week's journey.

Pardon me if I dwell for a moment upon the last interview which I had with him. It was a few weeks before his death, and on the occasion of a meeting of the board of trustees, called at his especial request. It was quite evident that his strength was not equal to the occasion. His utterance never appeared so difficult, and he even apologized by saying, "Don't be discomposed, Gentlemen; I do not suffer as much as I seem to." I cut short the work of the meeting as much as possible, as I saw that his strength was overtasked, and omitted several items of business that required attention. As soon as the adjournment was announced, I hastened to take him by the hand and bid him good-night. He grasped my hand, and, weak as he was, drew me to a chair by his side, and at once entered upon a clear and forcible argument upon the great questions which we had so often discussed. So earnest was he, that a moment's interruption by a member of the family seemed to annoy him. In his ardor to give expression to his thought, he seemed entirely forgetful of his bodily weakness. He was pushing his inquiries into those great subjects which we are assured the angels desire to look into, little thinking that the time was so near when

> "every bound should disappear,
> And infinite perfection close the scene."

From the nature of his complaints he had long expected that his last struggle would be one of great severity, and he awaited the summons with the most perfect calmness. For several months there were indications of failing strength, yet there was no abatement of heart or hope. The regular routine of business was attended to with few, if any, exceptions. On the evening of the 17th of June he attended to his correspondence as usual, though not without some inconvenience. After a restless night he woke at an early hour and asked for some refreshment. This not being in instant readiness, he fell into a quiet sleep, and to all appearance his wasted energies were recovering their accustomed strength. There was nothing to excite alarm even in the constant scrutiny and zealous watchfulness of filial love; and when his daughter approached his bedside, fearing that his sleep might be too protracted for his strength, she found that the great crisis was over, and that he had passed without a struggle and without a groan from the repose of sleep to the repose of death.

> "So fades a summer cloud away,
> So sinks the gale when storms are o'er;
> So gently shuts the eye of day,
> So dies a wave along the shore."

The character of Mr. Greene was one of remarkable scope, and, in endeavoring to sketch some of its prominent traits, I am greatly embarrassed in selecting my standpoint. There is indeed no one point from which we can readily catch all the features of interest that demand our attention. Intellectually considered, he was certainly gifted far above the average of men; and there seemed to be no sphere of purely intellective action in which he was not at home. His power of observation was such as must have given him a high rank as a philosopher had he chosen any department of physical or metaphysical science as the field of his action. As a manufacturer he not only mastered the principles of mechanics, as combined in all the machines which he had occasion to use, but he added to their efficiency from the resources of his own inventive powers. Had he been disposed, he might have claimed several patent rights on the basis of improvements which he had made in machinery. He also acquired an equal mastery of the principles of hydrostatics and hydraulics, and was able to criticise the standard works on these subjects in such a manner as to show that his knowledge was not drawn from books merely, but was the result of the independent action of his own mind. Indeed, he devoted much time and money to original investigation in these matters. United with his remarkable powers of accurate observation of facts was a no less remarkable power of combining them in their logical relations, and deducing from them the general principles and laws of which they were the individual expressions. It would be difficult to find in any of our periodicals a more critical examination of Tyndall's recent work on heat than he gave in a single sitting after reading it; nor have I seen a better exposition of Buckle's "History of Civilization" than he gave only a day or two after it was put into his hands. His power of concentration was really wonderful. By the mere exercise of his will, he seemed capable of directing all his intellectual powers to the investigation of a subject, and of holding them there at his pleasure. It was my privilege for some years to serve him somewhat in the capacity of a literary purveyor, and nothing surprised me more than the rapacity with which he devoured the contents of books. I well remember procuring for him a goodly octavo of vast learning, as well as of abstruse reasoning, which I handed to him with the familiar remark, "You have been rather clamorous for books of late, Mr. Greene; there is one which I think will last you for some time." It was not a week before, having occasion to call on him, I found the work had been mastered and laid aside. I have known him to dispose of an ordinary duodecimo at a single sitting.

He was evidently well versed in the principles of political economy, not in theory merely, but in their practical bearings; nor did he fail at all in applying these principles to new junctures and untried cases. The policy which he adopted as a manufacturer in the important crises of the last ten years was oftentimes in direct opposition to the judgment of a large proportion, if not indeed of a large majority of men engaged in the same department of business, as well as of those immediately associated with him. Yet the results showed the correctness of his reasoning, and the soundness of his conclusions.

His power of argumentation was seldom equalled, and rarely, if ever, surpassed. In addition to the qualities already mentioned, he possessed a remarkable grasp of intellect, which enabled him to bring all the points involved in a case of any complexity to their true relations and logical bearings. And when, in controverted matters, all the facts had been stated, and their importance duly considered, he rarely failed to carry conviction by his statement of the argument. In these features of his character it was easy to see the effect of his early legal training and the thoroughness with which he had mastered the principles of his profession. It was easy to see how unfortunate it was for his fame that he ever left it. Had he continued in its practice, he must have attained a reputation as an advocate and jurist second to none at the American bar. I should also mention that he possessed a remarkably exact and retentive memory. This enabled him to carry in his mind without difficulty all the circumstances relating to a particular case; it was a treasure-house from which he drew at will the materials of thought and argument. I have heard him repeatedly run through the genealogies of Matthew and Luke, and, without opening his Bible, point out all their discrepancies, and the modes of reconciling them. But I cannot take you over the entire field of his intellectual powers. It is too varied and extended for an evening's discussion. He could criticise the qualities of Sea-Island and middling upland cotton, and he could distinguish the Jehovistic and Elohistic sections of the Pentateuch; he could discuss the structure of the best form of the turbine wheel, and fortunate was that artist whose painting or whose sculpture revealed no defects to his just sense of the beautiful and the true. He would tell you all that was valuable in the last "Edinburgh Review," and he would give you a careful synopsis of the "Book of Wisdom," or of the "Gospel of Nicodemus." You would find him at one time exposing his health in tracing the path of a comet, and at another you would find him pointing out, from the observation of his naked eye, the error of an engineer in the grading of a street. He proved himself the master of the hardest financial problems of his time, and he walked with easy step among the highest mysteries of faith.

In passing from the intellectual to the moral features of his character, we find an expansion quite proportioned to the rank of these faculties in the spiritual framework. Here is the true sphere of manhood. Mere intellect, much as it is coveted, does not necessarily raise a man above a devil. In considering the moral qualities of Mr. Greene's character, all the elements of a noble manhood rise before us in majestic symmetry. Do courage and conscientiousness and will-power constitute essential elements of manhood, where shall we find them in fairer proportions? Or do we regard the kindlier qualities of benevolence, generosity, and the domestic virtues, in whom have they shone with a brighter lustre? Had he been a common sailor, he would have been the first to climb to the mast-head when the topsails were flying into ribbons; and had he been a common soldier, he would have been among the foremost, with steady nerve and unfaltering step, to enter the deadly breach spouting with fire. But to the dread trial of battle he was never called; yet he passed severer ordeals. John Milton tells, that

> "Peace hath her victories,
> No less renowned than war."

The facts would have borne him out in a still stronger statement. Many a spirit has stood unmoved amid showers of grape and canister, that has proved a mere poltroon in the emergencies of civic and business life.

The crisis never came that he hesitated to look calmly in the face; the man never lived whose eye could cause him to quail. To this high quality he owed much of his success. I believe there were many perilous junctures in his life, which served merely as healthful tonics to him, which would quite have crushed many a spirit esteemed capable and brave.* A few illustrations must

---

* I cannot forbear noticing here a striking resemblance between the character of Mr. Greene and of Messrs. Nathan and William Appleton.

"'I am not afraid,' was his reply to a friend, 'to tell you the truth; I believe I am not afraid of anything.'" — *R. C. Winthrop's Memoir of Hon. Nathan Appleton.*

"'I must be busy,' he said; 'I don't know how to stop. . . . I love best to do that which is the most difficult. . . . That which others would not undertake, pleases me most. . . . If my natural insight enables me to see farther than most men in certain directions, my nature also compels me to make use of this endowment. . . . I can't help seeing openings for profit, neither can I help availing myself of them. I pray God to keep me from being avaricious and proud of my success; but I cannot bear the shame of falling below my own powers, and being left behind by those who are not my equals.'"

"We are going rapidly into paper currency. Prices of all kinds of stocks and commodities will materially advance. I cannot avoid taking an interest in speculations, and taking advantage of the rise which I foresee. I am endeavoring to show the younger part of the merchants that an old merchant of seventy-five has faculties and energy left. *At the same time, I am thinking what I shall do with the profits on the pepper and saltpetre. I shall give part to the public, and part to destitute friends.*" — *Extracts from Memoir of Hon. William Appleton, by Rev. Chandler Robbins, D. D.*

"I sometimes think myself a hypocrite," said Mr. Greene to me on one occasion. "I sit here and converse upon stocks and cotton, and trade in general, with business men who call upon me in relation to these matters, and I suppose they think me interested in these subjects. But I am not; I mean to do my duty, but my heart is not in these matters."

It was some time subsequent to this, in the last months of 1861, I think, that I called on Mr. Greene, and found him unusually cheerful, with a glow upon his countenance which led me to say to him, "I am happy to see you appear so well this evening, Mr. Greene; you are better than usual, are you not?" "No," he replied, with a smile, "I don't know that I am. I pre-

suffice. I have already alluded to the great revulsion of 1857. I never saw him more playful, or apparently

sume I am a little excited; I have spent a hundred and fifty thousand dollars since Friday," (this was Tuesday,) "and I am quite provoked that they will not let me spend any more." He referred to the difficulty he experienced in getting his agents in New York and Boston to purchase cotton as rapidly as he desired.

Two intelligent manufacturers, speaking of these bold operations, said, "We were amazed at what seemed to us but reckless daring; we thought he was crazy; but he probably doubled his money in these transactions."

Some thirty years since, Mr. Greene made quite an extensive tour in the Southern States, and the tour was pretty fruitful in interesting incidents. At the end of a day's journey, in the thinly settled portions of North Carolina, the stage-coach in which he was travelling stopped at an inn, and the passengers, being quite overcome by the fatigues and dangers of the journey, were not disposed to proceed farther without a night's rest. There was a lady among the party in feeble health; and, in view of all the circumstances of the case, an urgent appeal was made to the driver to stop for the night. The driver was a man of a good share of what is termed physical courage, a fair specimen of the barbarism of that region, quite reckless, and fully determined to proceed. Mr. Greene, finding that the efforts of others had proved unavailing, determined to try his own powers of influence and persuasion, but with no better success. The driver declared that he would go on if it cost him his life, and was proceeding to prepare his horses for a start, when Mr. Greene, placing himself in his path, and fixing upon him a look that could not be mistaken, said, "I should be very sorry to kill you, sir; but if you touch those horses, I shall not hesitate a moment." The driver saw that he had found his match, and the party rested for the night.

While passing between two of the Southern ports in a sailing-packet, the vessel was overtaken by a severe gale, and to the imminent dangers from the storm were added those arising from a drunken captain. In this state of affairs the passengers felt that they must provide for their own safety, and they could only do this by making a change in the command of the vessel. It was proposed to place the mate in charge of the vessel, as the only way of saving their lives. This step was warmly advocated by Mr. Greene. Another passenger of less decision said to him, "Are you aware, sir, to what you are exposing yourself in advocating this measure; are you aware that you are liable to be hung?" "I should be very thankful," he replied, "for a reasonable chance of being hung; the prospect now is that we shall all soon be drowned."

The reader may be reminded of the remarks of John Foster: "In almost

more unconcerned. His activity, however, was surprising. He travelled hundreds, if not thousands, of miles,

all plans of great enterprise, a man must systematically dismiss at the entrance every wish to stipulate with his destiny for safety. He voluntarily treads within the precincts of danger; and though it be possible he may escape, he ought to be prepared with the fortitude of a self-devoted victim. This is the inevitable condition on which heroes, travellers, or missionaries among savage nations, and reformers on a grand scale, must commence their career. *Either they must allay their fire of enterprise, or abide the liability to be exploded by it from the world.*"

Let it not be thought that these and other incidents mentioned in preceding notes, which show the positive traits of Mr. Greene's character in so strong a light, are at all at variance with the milder virtues mentioned in the text. The upsetting of tables and counters, and the general rout and scourging of the profane and gambling crew that had placed their seats next the seat of God,

"and with cursed things
His holy rites and solemn feasts profaned,"

might not seem at first to harmonize with the spirit that cried, in the agony of dissolving nature, "Father, forgive them: they know not what they do;" the yearning for sympathy which prompted the seemingly timid and gentle rebuke, "What! could ye not watch with me one hour?" might at first view seem hardly consistent with the sublimest act of courage that the world has seen, and which palsied even the callous hearts of the Roman soldiers; yet both belong to the same character and to the same hour. Thus closely are united, in the great Exemplar of human virtue, the purest tenderness and the highest heroism.

Nor has Homer omitted to join

"The mildest manners with the bravest mind."

The tribute of Helen to the gentleness of Hector, in the last book of the *Iliad*, has been the admiration of all ages, and the author of " Tom Brown " has made one of the most interesting incidents in his hero's career to turn upon it.

"Hector, of all my brethren, dearest thou!
True, godlike Paris claims me as his wife,
Who bore me hither,—would I then had died!
But twenty years have passed since here I came
And left my native land; yet ne'er from thee
I heard one scornful, one degrading word;
And when from others I have borne reproach,
Thy brothers, sisters, or thy brothers' wives,

(no small matter for him in his state of health,) certainly not more in his own interest than in that of his friends. Most manufacturers at that time, with the interests involved in the management of more than thirty thousand spindles, found enough to occupy their attention in the conduct of their own affairs. It was otherwise with him. The panic of that period never shook his spirit. A commission-house in a distant city, to whom he had made large consignments, saw him one bright October morning entering their counting-room. "Well," says he, "you know what I have come for: I have come for money; how are you situated?" "Well, sir, we can pay you," was the reply. "But what is your condition?" he rejoined. "Comfortable, sir, now; though we cannot say where we shall be three months from this time." "Show me your balance-sheet." "We will do so in a few hours, if you will call again." Calling at the appointed time, he examined their balance-sheet, and said to them, "Gentlemen, don't you pay me a cent." "But, sir," said they, "the money is now due, and it is only your right and duty to take it; we cannot vouch for the future." "I did not ask your advice, gentlemen," he replied; "I shall not take a cent;" and so he left them. Hearing that another of his consignees was suffering under the terrible pressure, he hastened to his relief in person. Calling at his house in the early

> Or mother, (for thy sire was ever kind
> E'en as a father,) thou hast checked them still
> With kindly feeling and with gentle words.
> For thee I weep, and for myself no less;
> For through the breadth of Troy none love me now,
> None kindly look on me, but all abhor."
> *Earl of Derby's version.*

morning, before he had left for his counting-room, he placed in his hands a package containing forty thousand dollars. The surprised and grateful merchant protested against this generous act, as one of injustice to his noble friend's own interests; but his remonstrances were of no avail; he insisted upon his taking the money. Returning to Norwich, he sent him a hundred thousand dollars more, to be used as his necessities might require. This was all repaid in the course of a few months. "But," says the gentleman from whose letter I take the above facts, "the generosity of the whole transaction was such, it can never be effaced from my memory." "It may be proper to state," he adds, "that he had very little pecuniary interest in our concern, as we rendered an account of sales, and paid the amount every month, and of course we were very little indebted to him. I mention this to show that the course he pursued was not prompted by the fear of any pecuniary loss, but was simply the dictate of his noble and generous nature." Fearing that another commission-house whose paper he held to a considerable amount was in straitened circumstances, and not feeling that his slight personal acquaintance with them would justify his going to them himself, he hastened to a third party who was well acquainted with the firm in question, and, placing in his hands all their paper, requested him to go and assure his friends that their acceptances could be met entirely at their own convenience. Incidents of equal interest, illustrating his magnanimity and fortitude, might be gathered from the experience of our business men in Norwich. In this way did this heroic man go through that great financial hurricane. While others were taking in all sail, and running under bare poles, to use the nautical phrase, into the nearest and safest harbor, he spread every yard of canvas, and putting boldly out to sea in the very teeth of this terrible tornado, rode it out, and returned with not a mast sprung, or a sail rent, or a rope parted, laden not with the spoils which had been gathered on the breakers or in the quicksands, nor with living men whose fortunes had been rescued by a usurious redemption, but with the tributes of grateful hearts and devoted lives. He assured me that he never lost a cent in these transactions, even in a financial point of view; and at the close of the year following, 1858, he said he never expected to see so good a year again. Surely there is some truth in the sayings of those old worthies, now so little read, that there is a scattering that increaseth, and a withholding that tendeth to poverty, and that godliness is gain. "His history during this whole period under consideration," remarks one of his correspondents, "deserves to be written in letters of gold."

He met the great political crisis through which the nation is now passing with equal fortitude. He had fully considered the question at issue, and had predicted years ago that it would not be settled without an appeal to arms. But this conviction inspired no dismay, nor abated in the least the opposition which he had always felt and expressed to the great system of wrong which was so rapidly incorporating itself into the very framework of the government. As scene after scene in the great drama was unfolded, as State after State renounced its allegiance to the "best government which the world ever saw," his spirit rose with the demands of the times; and when the dread tocsin from Sumter sounded through the land, on the ever memorable 13th of April, he greeted it with something of the prophetic rapture which fired the soul of Samuel Adams, eighty-six years before, when, in an adjoining field, hearing the first volley from Lexington Common announcing that the great battle for liberty had begun, he threw up his arms and exclaimed, "Oh, what a glorious morning is this!" Preëminently a man of peace, and strongly opposed to war as a matter of principle, he nevertheless felt that the decisive hour had come. During the long and anxious winter months of 1860-61, he had feared that this great tempest of war was soon to burst upon the land; he feared much the material havoc and desolation of war, but he feared the moral degradation and shame of compromise more. He felt that the issue must be nobly met, or basely shunned. No man in the country had gauged the dimensions of the contest more accurately than he. "He knew it was an era, and he met it," to use the language of another,—"he met it with feelings like those of Luther, when he denounced the sale of indulgences, and pointed his thunders at once, poor Augustine monk, against the whole civil and ecclesiastical power of the Church, the Quirinal, and the Vatican. He braved the storm of war as Columbus braved the stormy billows of the glorious ocean, from whose giddy, curling tops he seemed to look out as from a watch-tower, to catch the first hazy wreath in the west, which was to announce that a new world was found. The poor Augustine monk knew and was persuaded that the time was come in which a mighty revolution was to be wrought in the Christian Church. The poor Genoese pilot knew in his heart that he had, as it were, but to stretch out the wand of his courage and skill, and call up a new continent from the depths of the sea;" and our departed friend beheld in the flames of Fort Sumter the beacon-light which heralded the return of the nation to the principles and practices of the fathers, and to the true spirit and genius of the Constitution. Through all the varying fortunes of the conflict he preserved the equanimity of his spirit: saddened, but not disheartened, by disaster; gladdened, but not transported, by success. When others were ready in their joy to proclaim the conflict ended, he saw that the war was yet in its earlier stages, and directed his business accordingly. It was my privilege frequently to be with him when the news of the day reached us in the afternoon papers; and he would sometimes ask me to take the paper and read over the chief topics of intelligence. I shall never forget, that, on one occasion, while yet the great question was undecided, as I read some items of interest from the army, he inquired if any progress was made towards the solution of the great political problem respecting the African race. I read to him all that the paper contained upon that aspect of the question, in which there was nothing of special encouragement. He threw himself back in his chair, and remained for some time absorbed in thought; then rising, with that expression of countenance which showed that all the great moral elements of his nature were in their highest action, yet perfectly self-possessed, he said, in tones of the deepest sorrow, "I had hoped that Mr. Lincoln would get his eyes opened before this time." Then, pacing his room, he remarked, with deep solemnity, "If I were forty years old, I would not be here." He soon resumed his seat, with a look which spoke with emphasis the great thought of Milton,—

> "God doth not need
> Either man's works or his own gifts. Who best
> Bear his mild yoke, they serve him best. His state
> Is kingly. Thousands at his bidding speed,
> And post o'er land and ocean without rest;
> They also serve who only stand and wait."

The whole scene was one not of interest merely: it was a true exhibition of the moral sublime. It was one of those occasions where a great soul imparts to action and to language a fulness and a depth of meaning far beyond what is contained in any or all of the lexicons. The words might have been uttered by many a trivial spirit, without producing any effect; but the action in this case was far beyond the reach of ordinary men. He seemed for the moment unreconciled to the lot to which his years and his infirmities consigned him, and like Achilles, when he looked out upon the field of conflict before Troy, and wished that the Greeks and Trojans might destroy each other, and make way for better men. He was, however, far from being censorious in his remarks upon the action of the administration. He well understood the difficulties of their position; he knew that it was far easier to criticise and complain than to plan and execute. He must, however, at times, I think, have experienced a feeling like that of La Grange, when he sighed to think that it had not fallen to his lot to be born in Newton's time, and have the first chance at the great problem of the universe. Conscious as he must have been of his ability to grapple with these great questions which have convulsed the world in our time,—questions that he so thoroughly understood, and the solution of which by the stern logic of events has followed so implicitly the logic of his reasoning,—the desire must have arisen in his mind, (as it certainly did in the minds of others,) not from vanity, but from virtue, that the force of his great abilities might be brought to bear on issues that have changed the course of our country's history. He knew, to use the bold figure of Macaulay, that it is the nature of the devil of tyranny to tear and rend the body which it leaves; but he regarded the convulsions of the terrible exorcism as of little account in comparison with the torments of perpetual possession. In regard to slavery, the commencement of the Rebellion found him just where it is hoped it will leave the nation. He had early studied this great system of wrong in theory and in its practical effects, in the Old and New Testaments, and on the Southern plantation.* He

---

* Reference has been made in a preceding note to a Southern tour which Mr. Greene made many years ago. His observations during this journey greatly strengthened his opposition to slavery.

It was, I think, while he was stopping at a public-house in Richmond, that the following incident occurred. A gentleman in Richmond, with the reputation of a good and kind master, owned a faithful and valuable slave, who had been promised, as a reward for his fidelity, that he should never be sold. But his master, becoming involved in debt, felt obliged to resort to the readiest means for raising the necessary amount, and this seemed to be to sell his faithful slave to a slave-broker from the far South. After concluding the bargain, and signing the papers, he called the slave to him and said, "John, I am sorry to inform you that such is my urgent need of money that I have been obliged to sell you; you have been a faithful servant, and I am very sorry to part with you; I hope you will fall into the hands of a

hated it in its whole history and philosophy with that perfect hatred which he bore to oppression and wrong at all times and under all circumstances. His charities were never more frequent or generous than to all objects that promised relief and encouragement to the African race. He was not noisy in the proclamation of his views upon this subject, nor did he hesitate for an instant to incur whatever reproach might be connected with an honest and manly statement of his con-

kind master." The negro dropped his head on receiving this announcement, and stood in silent sorrow for a moment; then, raising his eyes to his master, he replied, "I think, then, Massa, you ought to sell my wife with me." "I did not think of that," replied the master; "I had forgotten that you had a wife; but I will do so; your wife shall go with you." He called the broker, and stating to him the circumstance, requested him to buy the wife of the slave whom he had already purchased. The broker objected. He said the wife would only be an incumbrance, &c. "Then," said the master, "give up the bargain which we have just made." "No," he said, he should not do that; he had fairly bought and paid for his slave, and he should insist on the bargain. The poor master was helpless, and, calling again to him his former slave, informed him of the unavailing efforts which he had made to meet his wishes, and that he must go. The slave went directly into the back-yard, where stood a chopping-block, and taking the axe in his right hand, he cut off his left hand by a single stroke.

He travelled for some distance in Virginia in company with a planter of that region, who, finding that Mr. Greene was from a free State, was very ready to enlighten him upon the blessings of their peculiar civilization, dwelling with great earnestness upon the peaceful and happy condition of the slave population. In the course of their conversation the planter alluded to his own children, whom he spoke of with parental interest and solicitude. "I suppose you bring up your sons and daughters to the hardest labor, and in utter ignorance, do you not?" said Mr. Greene. "What do you mean, sir?" replied the planter; "do you mean to insult me, sir?" "Not at all, not at all, sir," rejoined Mr. Greene; "you show a father's interest and affection for your children, and I supposed you would certainly endeavor to secure for them what you have been representing as the happiest condition of human existence in the case of your slave population." The planter was silent.

victions. His history, in respect to this one question, would fill an interesting volume.

After what I have said, it is almost superfluous to remark that his moral sense was as delicate as his courage was strong. In all his transactions with other men, where his personal interests were involved, he was careful to regard their rights before his own. I have often heard the remark made, "If I wished to get an advantage of Mr. Greene, I would put myself completely in his power." In pecuniary transactions he has been known to pay thousands more than his judgment dictated was due, that he might not incur even the suspicion of unduly favoring his own interests. In one of the most trying junctures of his life he submitted his destiny entirely to the disposition of another party, and abided by their decision. In short, the moral faculty in his nature exercised the control to which its rank entitles it. The force of his nature was due not more to the strength of its individual elements than to their perfect correlation and subordination. Hence there appeared a remarkable symmetry in his character. There was no harsh or abrupt transition as you passed from its moral to its intellectual aspects. An equal power of will, with less of intellect and conscience, has produced a man of uncontrollable obstinacy; while an equally sensitive conscience, unguided by intellect, or not enforced by the requisite propelling power of the will, has resulted in nothing more than a well-meant feebleness and imbecility. In the exercise of these high qualities he exacted from his physical powers an amount of service that seemed incredible. Notwithstanding the careful husbandry of his strength, and the nice adjustment of his labors to times and circumstances, which he was compelled to observe, he continued, by his untiring energy, to work down men who regarded themselves as healthy and robust. An acquaintance of his who had known him forty years or more, writes me as follows: —

"I was frequently called on by Mr. Greene to visit the large mills in Lowell, Lawrence, and Fall River; and it was on these occasions that I became acquainted with his determined perseverance and great activity. In the hottest weather of July and August he would look over these large establishments from basement to attic, examining critically the machinery, and all new inventions and improvements. You know how slight he was. It seemed to me as though his strength could not hold out; but such was his energy and perseverance that I found it difficult to keep pace with him. And such seemed to be his course through life. I never knew a man more determined or more energetic."

I regret that it is not in my power to furnish some definite statistics illustrating the nature and extent of his benevolence; but he left no memoranda of his contributions to the various charities that shared in his generosity. He was a regular contributor to the great societies which have served as channels for Christian benevolence during the past fifty years; to none however, I think, was he more sincerely attached than to the American Peace Society. Truth, however, requires me to say that he had begun to feel some distrust in the colossal dimensions which these organizations were assuming; not that he thought less of their professed purposes, but because he feared that the real objects of these charities would be sacrificed to the magnificence of the machinery by which they are conducted. He knew well the dangers which beset voluntary associations when they have passed what we may term their heroic age. He knew that benevolence might become fashionable, and that fashionable giving was not Christian charity. None understood better than he the difference between the widow's mite and the sanctimonious offering of the purse-proud Pharisee. And he knew also that there are Pharisees in our own times, no less in numbers and no meeker in spirit than those that guarded the temple at Jerusalem against the heretical teachings of the young carpenter from Nazareth. He knew how easily and how imperceptibly an association which was Christian in its original method and purpose might be transformed into a mere propaganda of a sect, and that the real essence of Christian charity consists in bringing, as far as possible, the Christian man into personal and spiritual contact with his less favored brother in the true spirit of that language which he would often repeat with such touching pathos, " Inasmuch as ye have done it unto one of the least of these my brethren, ye have done it unto me." And this was the spirit that inspired all his charities. I have sometimes heard it said that it was no virtue in Mr. Greene to give, because his nature was so generous. This remark does him great injustice. It is true that his nature was generous, and that he was incapable of the close-fistedness that characterizes some men; but it is none the less true that his benevolence was the dictate of principle. I have known him to decline giving a dollar when the object for which it was solicited did not meet his approbation, and that, too, when he was incurring ill-will by refusing to give; and I have known him to give thousands unsolicited when he saw an occasion that seemed to him to demand it. From the *auri sacra fames,* the greed of gain, which eats like a gangrene into so many natures and utterly destroys every principle of true manhood, he was entirely free. When such cases were brought to his notice, he would speak of them with as much sorrow and in the same manner as he would speak of cases of intemperance or any other form of vicious indulgence.

The qualities which I have noticed, you must have observed, are those which, in connection with some others, constitute the basis of the strongest and warmest friendships. The principles on which he founded his friendships were far different from those which enter into the composition of that which often passes under the name. "I have no fellowship," he once remarked, "for the commonly received maxim that business is one thing and friendship another." "If," he continued, "a man is my friend, I have a right to go to him in my necessity; and I should think little of my friendship for a man, if he did not feel at liberty to come to me for assistance in his time of need:" and, strange to say, not a half-hour had elapsed after he made this remark before application was made to him for a loan of five hundred dollars for a friend, which he at once granted, with far more apparent pleasure than if it had been invested in a form which promised a speculative profit. The holidays, as they are called, the week between Christmas and New Year's, he used to term his Saturnalia; and he claimed the privilege at this season, as he said, of treating his friends just as he saw fit, without any right of redress on their part. The nature of this treatment you can infer from the following note which I have been permitted to copy.

"NORWICH, *Jan.* 1.

"MY DEAR BROTHER, —

"There is one day of all others in the year which I regard more particularly as my own, and therefore on which I the more like to have my own way, and I think it would not be kind in you to oppose me. One year since I hardly thought I should live to see this day, and to unite with my friends here in mutual kind wishes which the day so appropriately suggests. But the Lord has continued me here until now. What all his purposes are in so doing I know not. But I trust they are for good, and I think one of them I know. He says to me, You hold a certain bond of my brother; have I not paid it? Even so, Lord Jesus, in thy name, blessed forever, I send it unto him.*

"In the bonds of love, and I hope humbly of Christian brotherhood,
"Yours,
"WM. P. GREENE."

On another occasion he said to a friend, whose tears bore witness to the depth of his gratitude for the favor he was receiving, "Don't be disturbed, sir; I am only doing for you what I know you would do for me, were our circumstances reversed; I may need your aid yet." And so I might continue for an hour. When he knew a friend was in need, he oftentimes did not wait for him to come for aid: he sought him out, and when he had relieved his wants, he left him a free man. He was careful not to wound one's self-respect by striving to make him feel that he had received a great favor which should be held in lasting remembrance. On the contrary, he strove to lighten the load of obligation which his kindness could not but inspire. Some of his noblest

---

* This letter enclosed obligations to the amount of more than two thousand five hundred dollars.

acts were performed in an indirect and playful way, and he seemed rather to shun than to court the expressions of thankfulness to which they gave rise. When, however, a token of gratitude was handed to him as a recognition of obligation for some previous favor, he received it in such a way as to assure the giver that he highly prized the attention that was shown him. But by far the greater portion of these generous deeds were known only to the recipients and to his God. What I have mentioned are only a few of the flowerets that have been casually gathered along the pathway of his life.

In social intercourse he exhibited superior powers of conversation, and very few subjects could be mentioned which he was not qualified to discuss. He greatly enjoyed earnest and friendly contact with other minds, and was delighted to find himself ably confronted in argument. He would sometimes espouse the weak side of an argument for the purpose of testing the strength of his opponent, always contriving, however, to let him know before concluding the views which he actually held. A clergyman, a stranger to him, once called on him to solicit a contribution for an important object. Without noticing the request, he began at once in all apparent seriousness to assail the cause for which aid was solicited, and thus put the applicant on the defensive. Surprised by the vehemence with which his cause was attacked by a man from whom much aid had been expected, he made an elaborate defence, and was not sparing in his exhortations and warnings against fatal errors and damnable heresies. The result was the very unexpected reception of a donation twice as large as he had anticipated, with the kind remark that, as he had defended his cause so well, he was entitled to that. Applicants for charity were frequently subjected to pretty serious cross-questioning in this way; and from them, as well as from other sources, he derived a very accurate knowledge of the various charities before the Christian public.

In the lighter forms of conversation, in sallies of wit and humor, he was always at home. But entertaining as he ever showed himself in these respects, his preference was for the more serious subjects in social discussion. He was able to make one feel perfectly at home in his society; and though his manners were dignified and refined, and even courtly when the occasion required, his habit was to renounce all mere mannerism, and both to observe himself and encourage in others that cordial and familiar freedom and ease which no system of etiquette can secure, and no formal conventionalism can compass. What Pope has said of style in writing applies with striking force to his style of social and friendly intercourse: —

> "Great wits may sometimes gloriously offend,
> And rise to faults true critics dare not mend;
> From vulgar bounds with brave disorder part,
> And snatch a grace beyond the reach of art,
> Which, without passing through the judgment, gains
> The heart, and all its end at once attains."

Few people in Norwich who knew Mr. Greene are without their fund of anecdotes illustrative of the simplicity and cordiality, and at the same time of the peculiarity, of his habits of social intercourse.

But there yet remains for our consideration the highest and fairest portion of his character.

The Christian is the highest style of man, and it is in its Christian aspects that Mr. Greene's constitution invites the closest scrutiny and presents its greatest strength. Perhaps, indeed, I have been contemplating the elements of his nature in an inverted order. It might have been better for me to have regarded the great qualities which we have been considering as the outgrowth of the deep Christian convictions on which they rested. But it has seemed to me preferable to take our last view of the man from the battlements and bastions that command his entire character. His religious development partook strongly of the individuality that marked the whole life. In giving a brief sketch of him as a Christian, I deem it a sacred duty, so far as I am able, to present the man as he actually was. There is a morbid sensitiveness in some minds which hesitates to state with frankness any view which deviates from the standards of a generally received orthodoxy. It is felt by some that any deviation from the creed or the rubric, however pure or devout the life which accompanies it may be, is just so far an abatement from the integrity of Christianity, and hence encouraging what is termed a dangerous tendency. Such religionists, had they written the evangelical records, would never have mentioned the doubts of Thomas, the lapses of Peter, and the noble contentions of Paul with his fellow-apostles. The eminently human, and consequently instructive, features of these narratives would have had some of their most valuable lessons sacrificed to a tame conformity to the decretals of some council at Jerusalem, by which the virtues and the failings of every individual believer would have

been rounded into ethical propriety and theological
soundness. But inasmuch as those evangelists wrote
not for a sect or a party or a system, but simply to
perpetuate in human lives the life of the Master, there
are found many loose ends and rough corners which
have sorely perplexed theological architects for these
eighteen centuries. I make these remarks, not because
I am about to startle you by the announcement of
some monstrous heresy, but because the faith of our
lamented friend was rather Christian than theological.
It is expressed more accurately in the words of the
great Teacher himself, as recorded by the fourth evan-
gelist, " Believe in God and believe in me," * than in
the creeds of Augustine and Athanasius. His religious
faith was preëminently Christian; and his seeming
rejection of what some men regard as cardinal points
of doctrine was due rather to the wider range of
his views resulting from profound study of the sacred
Scriptures, and to his further advance in the divine life,
than to any denial of fundamental truths. Placing
himself boldly and firmly upon the foundation of the
Apostles and Prophets, with Jesus Christ himself as
the chief corner-stone, he felt that the whole series of
councils, synods, confessions, creeds, and platforms, were
only so far binding upon him as their results were
based upon the teachings of the inspired Word. To
those who rest content in a limited number of dogmas
as comprising the sum total that is known or can be
known of the great salvation that was wrought by
Jesus, and who find in these dogmas a refuge for their

---

* This is both Campbell's and Norton's version of John xiv. 1, and is
without doubt the true rendering.

ignorance and an apology for their indolence, as well as a pardon for their sins, the views which he entertained would seem lax and heretical. It is true that he, in common with the leading theological thinkers of this century, reached, as the result of patient and prayerful study, conclusions rather negative than positive. In his earlier religious life he felt it his duty to follow without questioning the prescriptions of ecclesiastical and theological authority. He trod with exemplary patience the weary rounds of the metaphysical treadmills in which so many have wasted their lives, and he toiled at those enigmas which have puzzled hundreds of generations, and will puzzle hundreds more. From these spiritual toils — which Lord Macaulay so aptly compares to the labors of the damned in the Grecian Tartarus, spinning forever on the same wheel round the same pivot, gaping forever after the same deluding clusters, pouring water forever into the same bottomless buckets, pacing forever to and fro on the same wearisome path after the same recoiling stone — he rose at length to a higher and simpler and more confiding faith in the Father through the Son. He preferred to listen to the Sermon on the Mount, to catch the words of spirit and life that were spoken to the fishermen of Galilee, the woman of Samaria, and the mourners of Bethany, rather than to talk of election, reprobation, and final perseverance. Nor did he less delight in the sterner lessons which were given by the great Teacher of mankind. The pregnant woes pronounced against a corrupt hierarchy in his last visit to the Temple, the mournful predictions of impending wrath which were uttered from the side of Olivet, the moral heroism of Stephen, and the manly self-defences of Paul in almost every city of the known world,—all these and their kindred scenes received a reverent welcome from his great spirit, and found in him a sympathy which few are able to accord to them.

He possessed in an eminent degree that rare quality which we may term intellectual sincerity, the ability to examine any theory or any principle with perfect candor and impartiality. He understood perfectly the difference between defending a position and examining it; and that in religious matters men often think they are seeking for truth, when they are only erecting defences around what they have already decided to be truth. This sincerity of which I have spoken will often assume the appearance of a cold indifference to the enthusiastic partisan and sectarian. Such was the case with Mr. Greene. Many who conversed with him on religious subjects left him with the impression that he was indifferent or hostile to the truth, simply because he could see and feel the force of objections which they either could not or would not consider. The presence of a clear and penetrating intellect seemed to them to indicate the absence of a warm and devout heart. The fearlessness with which he examined the most cherished articles of their belief appeared to them almost like an irreverent intrusion into forbidden sanctities. The perfect liberty which he had found in Christ reverently to examine all things, whether Paul, or Apollos, or Cephas, or the world, or life, or death, or things present, or things to come, could hardly seem otherwise than profane to those who seldom or never question the traditions of the fathers, or trouble themselves with the higher verities of the Christian faith. He had little patience with the timid conservatism so often met with, which trembles for the stability of the whole temple of truth, because some resolute worshipper insists upon removing some of the rubbish which in the progress of centuries has gathered in its sacred courts, and defiled its hallowed altars. Nor did he, to change the figure and adopt the language of another, regard with much favor that "skeptical credulity of feeble-minded piety, which dreads the cutting away of an orthodox misbelief as if the life-blood of faith would follow, and would keep even a stumbling-block in the way of salvation, if only generations enough have tripped over it to make it venerable." He believed that there is nothing so indestructible as truth; and since the eternal years of God are hers, he felt assured that the clouds and mists which ignorance and bigotry, or false friends or open enemies, might raise, would soon disappear before her brightness, as the mists of the morning before the rising sun. He was accordingly always found in the vanguard of the religious thinkers of the age; and as he knew that the excessive ardor of the valiant soldier is more easily forgiven than the sloth and cowardice of the straggler, he preferred to share in the dangers of the front, rather than in those of the rear; to join in the first shout of triumph on the enemy's ramparts, rather than expose himself to the dangers of the pursuing foe; to hazard, in a steady adherence to the great Master, all the horrors and honors of the cross, rather than enjoy the safety and shame of the straggling Peter. He knew that the heresies of indolence and cowardice were far greater than those of industry and courage; that in things spiritual as in things temporal, in Church as in State, in the individual mind as in the associated minds of a whole community, the dangers of activity and enterprise bear no proportion to those of sloth and stagnation. In short, as it was in the great tragedy of Gethsemane, so it has always been; a period of sloth and sleep betrays the Son of Man into the hands of sinners; the conservative and thoughtless disciples enjoyed their quiet slumbers, while their solitary Master was sweating blood.

I scarcely need add, after making these remarks, that he took the liveliest interest in the questions which now agitate the thinking portion of the Christian world. He was not simply well informed upon the points at issue, but attained that mastery of them which is only surpassed by those who have made these subjects their specialty. He manifested great eagerness to get hold of every volume pertaining to either side of these controversies. He followed the fortunes of Dr. Davidson and the Bishop of Natal with lively interest, not so much from entire sympathy with their views, as because he esteemed them honest men; and he felt keenly the disgrace that was brought upon the Christian name in heaping upon them, as was done in some quarters, personal abuse, instead of meeting them with manly courtesy and scholarly logic. He believed that God had sent his Son into the world, that the world through him might be saved; and he had no fears that Bishop Colenso and the Oxford scholars would defeat the plan, and compel its abandonment.

A clergyman of high standing and extensive influence, who had known Mr. Greene for twenty years or more, and had had frequent occasion to call upon him, thus writes me in regard to his views of his character:—

"I well recollect being very forcibly struck with his strongly marked individuality, with the versatility and vigor of his powers, with the freshness and originality of his views on almost every subject, and with the accuracy, minuteness, and extent of his knowledge. In all my acquaintance with men of talent and culture, I can recall scarce one that impressed me so deeply in these respects; and seldom if ever did I retire from one of these interviews without feeling my inferiority, and my obligations for the most valuable thoughts which he had given me. I could not help wondering how a man of such frail and precarious health, and with an amount of business on his hands sufficient to tax a frame of iron and nerves of steel, came to have at ready command such a fund of various and profound knowledge on almost every conceivable topic. I can hardly give particulars, but cannot refrain from alluding to one or two. In one interview we happened to touch upon the Book of Job; and I was surprised to find him so familiar — more than one clergyman in a hundred — with the history, character, and peculiar difficulties of that singular production. He extemporized a learned disquisition that would have done credit even to a professor of sacred literature in one of our theological seminaries. At another time the subject of modern spiritualism came up; when I found him ready at once to dissect and expose its pretensions with the keen discrimination and knowledge of facts and principles that you would expect only from an adept in philosophy and natural science."

Another gentleman of high intelligence, who had known him for thirty years, while conversing with me quite enthusiastically in regard to his character, exclaimed, upon my alluding to his knowledge on biblical subjects, "Yes, he used to knock me about like a shuttlecock." He always kept his Greek Testament and lexicon by his side, and though he made no pretensions to what is now termed accurate Greek scholarship, he was able to form a correct estimate of the critical labors of others upon the original text. He was not content with our common English version; he had always at hand the Septuagint, with the other most approved translations of the Old and New Testaments. He was also well acquainted with the Apocryphal writings, and the Apostolic Fathers. He studied these as side-lights to the canonical Scriptures, and drew from other collateral sources to an extent quite remarkable for a layman. I must not forget to mention that he indulged himself but seldom in the expression of his devotional feelings; he inclined much more in conversation to dwell upon those topics which concern our relations to God, and the interpretation of the Scriptures. This apparent reserve led me for some time to fear that he had neglected the culture of the affections, in his deep devotion to the more speculative aspects of religious truth. But this I found to be a great mistake. The fervor of his feelings was fully proportioned to the extent of his religious knowledge; and I speak what I know, when I affirm that his habits of devotion were regular, and his communion with his Maker intimate and constant. He avoided the free use of language so commonly employed in social religious intercourse, from the conviction that these expressions often indicate the absence rather than the presence of true devotional feeling. He abhorred cant on all subjects, and especially in religion. His yea was yea, and his nay was nay, and language with him was the vehicle, not the substitute, for thought and feeling. By far the highest exhibition of faith and resignation I ever witnessed, was in an hour's interview with him on his return from the grave of her who for forty years had trod the paths of life by his side, and whose virtues he seemed at a loss for words fitly to describe.

If to do justice and to love mercy, if clean hands and a pure heart, if visiting the fatherless and widows in their affliction, and keeping himself unspotted from the world, if love to God, and love to man as God's creature, of whatever rank, complexion, or condition, if an humble and childlike faith in Jesus as the great manifestation of the Father,—if these, or any other tests which may be gathered from the inspired Word, constitute any criterion of Christian character, he certainly, whatever may have been his views of the systems of Rome, of Oxford, or Geneva, was entitled to this greatest of all names.

I have thus touched upon some of the prominent points of the character which we have met this evening to commemorate. But I feel, as those of you who really *knew* him must also feel, how far I have failed to present the man. No one can realize more deeply than I do how far my dull mosaic falls below the reality of the life which a few months ago was passing among us as a stream of beneficent beauty and power. But what rhetoric or what sculpture can worthily exhibit so grand a reality? What language can properly speak the music of that voice which trembled with tenderness and love, or the expression of that eye when moistened with tears of affection, or the overwhelming power of that manner when he changed to sterner moods? The majesty of that presence in which no one might trifle, the benignity with which he conferred a favor, the humor with which he provoked your laughter, the warm sympathy with which he made another's grief his own, the loathing, withering scorn with which he looked upon every form of falsehood and deceit, the resistless force of his logic,— all these indeed may be sketched individually, but not as a united and harmonious whole. These high qualities in their due relation and reciprocal action exhibited a harmony, a strength, and a grandeur of character as far above the best pictures of language as the speaking life is above the motionless features of the silent canvas.

To some, the views which I have taken may seem exaggerated: I *know* them to be tame. But such, I apprehend, were really unacquainted with the man, or fail to comprehend the important truth that private, no less than public life, has its heroes, and that their heroism is none the less real because it is not set off to the view by any of the attractions of official station. We must not forget the often-quoted remark of De Tocqueville, the most philosophical writer on American society and institutions, that nothing surprised him more than the wealth of talent in this country in private life, and its poverty in public life. It is precisely here that we see the real greatness of Mr. Greene's character. Possessing all the elements of a great political leader, (unless, indeed, it be thought that he lacked that moral flexibility which the exigencies of political life are sometimes thought to require,) he yet chose to remain undistinguished in the ranks of the humblest citizenship, content with realizing, so far as possible, his own ideas of excellence, and diffusing their influence in the community. As I retired from some of those interviews which it was my privilege often to have with him, those choice and blessed hours when the world and its interests were forgotten, and he unconsciously fell into his happiest strains of colloquial discussion, when the course of his thoughts seemed like the flow of a majestic river,—

> "Though deep, yet clear; though gentle, yet not dull;
> Strong without rage; without o'erflowing, full;"

while I pondered upon the great lessons which he drew from the past, his ready solution of the problems of the present, and his almost oracular predictions of the future, I was often reminded of the lines of Coleridge,—

> "How seldom, friend! a good great man inherits
> Honor or wealth, with all his worth and pains!
> It sounds like stories from the land of spirits,
> If any man obtain that which he merits,
> Or any merit that which he obtains.
>
> "For shame, dear friend! renounce this canting strain!
> What wouldst thou have a good great man obtain?
> Place — titles — salary — a gilded chain —
> Or throne of corses which his sword hath slain? —
> Greatness and goodness are not means, but ends!
> Hath he not always treasures, always friends,
> The good great man? — three treasures, love and light,
> And calm thoughts, regular as infant's breath;
> And three firm friends, more sure than day and night, —
> Himself, his Maker, and the angel Death."

I have seen two of the chief magistrates of the nation, the one in his career of triumph through the towns and cities of the land, the guest of legislative and academic bodies, and, for the time, the very cynosure of the popular gaze, the other dispensing in the

Executive mansion the honors of the nation to learned and diplomatic bodies, in all the pomp and circumstance of the highest official station; the first now fills a traitor's grave, the second is running the last sands of life in an obscurity from which not even his friends would recall him; and I have seen William P. Greene in the retirement of his study and counting-room, directing with beneficent wisdom the industrial life of whole communities, dispensing in copious showers and gentle dews the bounty which his talents and energy had acquired, holding high converse with the good and great of all ages, " aloof from the competitions and the prizes, the mean jealousies, the hollow pretences, the brutal vilifyings, the base intrigues, and the measureless corruptions of public life, looking down from the serene height of his consistency and his principles, upon their paltry ambition and its more paltry rewards."

But let us contemplate for a moment the results of the life which we have been considering. What is its import and significance to the generation and the community to which it belonged? What is its rank among human lives? Lord Bacon, in his essay upon Honor, has given us the degrees of both "sovereign" and "subject" honor; and first in the scale of sovereign honor he has placed what he terms the "*conditores imperiorum*," or founders of States, and as illustrations of this order of greatness has mentioned Romulus and Cyrus and Cæsar; then come the "*legislatores*," or lawgivers, the second founders of States; and to these succeed the "*salvatores*," or deliverers; and in the fourth place the "*propugnatores imperii*," or warriors who enlarge their country's boundaries; and lastly, the "*patres patriæ*," or fathers of their country. The several degrees of honor in the subject or citizen he characterizes as, first, the "*participes curarum,*" or prime ministers; second, the "*duces belli,*" or great captains; third, the "*gratiosi,*" or favorites, those who, *without doing any harm to mankind, have been successful in pleasing their sovereigns* (a singular order of merit surely; we should suppose that court-jesters and court-fools are referred to*); and lastly, the "*negotiis pares,*" the ministers of State. In all these degrees of honor we find no place for him whose loss we deplore; no, nor even for Lord Bacon himself in that aspect of his character for which alone he would thank mankind to remember him. Lord Bacon, the philosopher, the great founder of modern science, could not, as I see, be ranked in any of these degrees which he has arranged to comprise all the orders of sovereign and subject merit. Far different was the estimate of the great Roman poet. In the Elysian fields, in communion with poets and heroes, with the founders of States, with Orpheus, Ilus, and Dardanus, has he fixed the abodes of

---

* If Dr. John Doran's somewhat irreverent suspicion be worthy of notice, the claims of court-jesters to the honors of the *gratiosi* are not to be treated lightly. In the supplementary chapter to his *History of Court-Fools*, published in the *Book of Days*, Dr. Doran says: "There are four years of Shakspeare's life (1585-9) during which nothing is known of his whereabouts. In a letter addressed by Sir Philip Sidney from Utrecht, 1586, to his father-in-law, Walsingham, there is a passage to this effect, — ' I wrote to you a letter by *Will*, my Lord of Leicester's *jesting-player.*' Who was this jesting-player? He may have been Will Johnson, Will Sly, Will Kimpe, or, as some have thought, even the immortal William himself." If Lord Bacon had derived his ideas of favorites from such men as William Shakspeare, it is not surprising that he has placed them one degree above the "ministers of State." But Shakspeare's feats as jesting-player had better be treated under the same head as his exploits in deer-stealing, — Shakspearean Mythology.

> "Searching wits of more mechanic parts,
> Who graced their age with new-invented arts." *

And who will not say that in this instance the inspiration of the poet transcends the wisdom of the philosopher?

Lord Bacon wrote in the palmiest days of the Tudor and Stuart dynasties, when the great forces of the human mind had already shaken the spiritual despotisms of the Continent, and were soon to burst with explosive violence beneath the throne of England's king; he wrote at a time when the human mind had already become weary of the old *Organon* of Aristotle, and the senseless jargon of the schoolmen, and was waiting for a new dispensation in science, which the great Chancellor himself was destined to inaugurate; he wrote at a time when kings ruled by divine right, and subjects rebelled at the risk not only of civil but ecclesiastical censure, when rank was omnipotent and manhood lightly esteemed. Had he written in our day; could he behold the wonderful change in human affairs which his philosophy has wrought, — how kings have declined, and subjects risen in importance; could he see the great results that have flown from his new method, from observation and experiment, from the application of the great forces of nature to the whole sphere of human wants; could he, I say, behold all this, he would revise his scales of honor; he would at least make provision for himself in his orders of merit; he would

---

* " Hic manus ob patriam pugnando vulnera passi,
Quique sacerdotes casti, dum vita manebat,
Quique pii vates, et Phœbo digna locuti,
Inventas aut qui vitam excoluere per artes,
Quique sui memores alios fecere merendo."

make provision not only for the royal names of Newton and Leibnitz, but also for the Arkwrights and Fultons, the Hargreaveses and Whitneys, and a host of philosophers and inventors who have arisen under the stimulus which he gave to human thought. Could he contrast the England of to-day with the England over which the Tudors reigned, and see all the great discoveries and generalizations and applications, from the great induction of Newton to the last equally grand generalization of the philosophers of the Royal Institution; could he take in at one view the highest and most abstruse teachings of the Royal Society, and follow these through all their applications to meet the wants and elevate the condition of the humblest peasant; could he see more work done in a single day and in a single mill in Manchester than was done in the whole kingdom of Elizabeth in a month; could he glance at the last half-century of our New-England history, and see how, from the moral courage and inventive genius of comparatively few men, — the Slaters, the Lowells, the Jacksons, the Lawrences, the Appletons, and the Greenes, — our sterile soil has become dotted with manufacturing cities and villages, how the wilderness and solitary place have been glad for them, and the desert has rejoiced and blossomed as the rose; could he see how all the bright visions of his fancy in the "New Atlantis" have here become the sober realities of history, that within the compass of a single generation a city founded on the banks of the Merrimack has grown to greater importance than Rome had attained when she drove out the Tarquins, that the spinning and weaving of a single week in Lowell would have supplied the whole empire of Augustus for half a lifetime, — he might have found, for the names I have mentioned, a place as honorable as he has accorded to the leader of vagabonds and fugitives who settled on the slopes of the Palatine.

Yes, Ladies and Gentlemen, when the history of this country in this century shall be written in the spirit in which Macaulay has recorded the history of England, when the progress and condition of the people, the real sovereigns of our land, shall be faithfully stated, it will be seen that the foundations of our greatness and strength were laid, not by families that came in with the Conqueror, not by the heirs of the old European despotisms, nor by the offshoots from the crumbling houses of their nobilities, but by plebeian minds and plebeian hands; not by the blood of the Cavaliers were nourished the sinewy arms that have smitten the hydra of Rebellion as with the club of Hercules, but by the stern old Saxon, which courses as briskly through our veins as it did in those of Egbert and Alfred. Not from the baronial castles and tapestried halls of England's proud names are derived the patents of our nobility, but from our farms, our cotton and woollen mills, and our machine-shops. In these, not in our arsenals and armories, nor even in our banks, are the real hidings of the nation's power. Our greasy mechanics (let us accept this term of insult, and make it as honored in the world's history as our fathers made those of Puritan and Roundhead) can show in our Patent-Office, as the products of their achievements, devices more expressive and blazonry more brilliant than are found in all the records and emblems of heraldry.

When the sons and daughters of Norwich gathered, a few years since, to celebrate their bicentennial jubilee, our honored friend flung to the breeze, from his modest family mansion, as his armorial ensign, a goodly length of cotton cloth, with the motto, "NOT ASHAMED OF HIS OCCUPATION;" and well might he glory in an occupation in the pursuit of which he had been able to do more for Norwich than any other man who ever lived here,— in which he did for this city what Boott and Jackson did for Lowell, the Lawrences for Lawrence;—well might he glory in an occupation which places him in the front rank of our New-England nobility.

When the antiquaries of the next century shall investigate the etymologies of the names of our industrial cities, they will not be obliged to do as a modern author has done, who spent

"a hundred leaves
To prove his ancestors notorious thieves;"

nor will they find them based upon any of the myths of Greek and Roman fable, nor upon the equally imaginary achievements of mediæval feudalism. They will trace them to the triumphs of honorable and intelligent men over the forces of nature, to the devolving upon natural agencies the exhausting toil that had previously been performed by human hands. One of the twelve labors of Hercules, which has gained immortal renown, was the turning of the streams of Alpheus and Peneus from their channels to cleanse the stables of Augeas. What shall we then say of our modern Heraclidæ, who have turned our rivers and rivulets from their natural channels, where from the morning of creation they had flowed in idle splendor or thundered in useless magnificence, to wake the music that attends the march of our great civilization, by mingling in sweet accord the roar of the waterfall with the click of the shuttle and the hum of the spindle; who have entered the secret places of the Most High, not, like Prometheus, to *steal* the fire of heaven, but in filial confidence to take it with our Father's approval and scatter its blessings to all the children of his care; who have disarmed the lightnings of their terrors, and made them the readiest servants of mankind; who have evoked from water, as liquid or vapor, a productive force equal to that of the entire population of the globe;* who have brought to the humblest cottage comforts and even luxuries which a century since were unknown in the palaces of kings? These, these are the true *conditores imperiorum*, — they who have lived and toiled, not for a family, a clan, a party, or a nation; not the Tudors nor Plantagenets, the Warwicks nor Wolseys; not Guelphs nor Ghibellines, not Hapsburgs nor Bourbons; not those who have set up thrones or founded dynasties; but those who have extended the dominion of man farther into the great domain of Nature, and taught the humblest peasant-boy to "bind the sweet influences of Pleiades" and wield the forces that " guide Arcturus with his sons."

Nor is it merely in ministering to the physical wants of mankind that these pioneer manufacturers have

---

* It has been estimated that the amount of labor performed by the aid of machinery in England alone is equal to that of between three and four hundred millions of men by direct labor. If to this be added the labor performed by machinery on the Continent and in America, there can be no doubt that the sum total will be equal to that of one thousand millions of men, or the entire population of the globe. — *Buckland's Geology*, Vol. I. p. 494; *Ruggles's Address to the Alumni of Yale College.*

earned their claims to our remembrance and gratitude. No men in this country have done more to promote the higher culture, — the improvement of the mind and the heart. The school-house and the church have been the constant attendants of the cotton-mill. The schools of Greeneville (thanks to Mr. William H. Coit and his coadjutors) were pronounced, years ago, by the highest authority, the best of their grade in the State. Nor have they forfeited this honorable distinction; others may have come into line, but they have not been distanced in the race for excellence. The greater portion of the funds of the Free Academy were earned upon the two streams that flow upon either side of it. The eponyms of our manufacturing cities and villages are to a great extent the same as those of our academic and university halls. The family name which is borne by the metropolitan city of the New-England arts is the same that is borne by the Lowell Institute, the largest and noblest charity that the City of the Puritans can boast. When in the world's history has it fallen to the lot of father and son to share more worthily in honors more heartily bestowed?* The father has

---

* Francis C. Lowell has claims upon the grateful remembrance of his countrymen, which have been but partially recognized. Though born to affluence, and encountering all the obstacles that affluence presents to usefulness, he nevertheless originated and perfected inventions and improvements which have left their impress upon the age. He appears to have possessed the highest order of mathematical talent united with the rare power of directing it to the most successful practical results. Though not a professed politician, his clear insight in industrial and commercial affairs gave him an easy ascendency over the minds of such men as William Lowndes and John C. Calhoun; and, as has been mentioned on a preceding page, he induced these statesmen to inaugurate the "minimum duty," which lay at the foundation of the American protective system. He was, however, no blind advocate for protection, but appears to have been opposed to a tariff

given to his country one of the most effective machines that minister to human comfort, and started his countrymen in a new career of industrial and civilized life. The son, impelled by his interest in all that pertains to human welfare to visit every region of the globe and every condition of human society, finds himself arrested by disease on the banks of the Nile; and there, amid the crumbling monuments of Egyptian grandeur, surrounded by pyramids, catacombs, temples, and sphinxes, impressed, as it would seem, with the utter failure of all material forms to gain that immortality which these cyclopean masses were reared to secure, he seats himself upon the top of a palace of the Pharaohs, with the gloomy magnificence of Karnak and Luxor in full view, to found in his native city, by the royal gift of two hundred and fifty thousand dollars, an institution whose home should not be found in piles of gorgeous architecture,* but in the minds and hearts of men, to diffuse

of high duties. It was at the cotton mill of the Boston Company, under his direction at Waltham, Massachusetts, that all the operations for converting the raw material into salable goods were first performed under the same roof. Mr. Calhoun visited this mill in 1818, and apparently derived great satisfaction from witnessing its operations.

It is also to Mr. Lowell that we are indebted, more than to any other man, for the great moral superiority of our manufacturing cities and villages over those of the Old World. He was deeply impressed with the degraded condition of the manufacturing population of England, and wisely determined to guard against similar abuses in this country.

* The Lowell Institute, established by the munificence of John Lowell, Jr., is sacredly guarded, by a stipulation in the will of its founder, against the architectural abuses which have ruined the prospects of so many ample charities. I cannot resist the temptation to quote the remarks of Sir Charles Lyell upon Mr. Lowell's bequest, and upon the general subject of architecture in connection with educational charities.

"Mr. John Lowell, a native of Massachusetts, after having carefully studied the educational establishments of his own country, visited London in 1833, and having sojourned there some months, paying a visit to the Univer-

through the world and down the ages the arts of an enlightened philosophy and the principles of a Christian morality.

sity of Cambridge and other places, he pursued his travels in the hope of exploring India and China. On his way he passed through Egypt, where, being attacked, while engaged in making a collection of antiquities, by an intermittent fever, of which he soon afterwards died, he drew up his last will in 1835, amidst the ruins of Thebes, leaving half of his noble fortune for the foundation of a literary institute in his native city. . . . . When it is stated that the fees of the Lowell Institute at Boston are on a scale more than three times higher than the remuneration awarded to the best literary and scientific lecturers in London, it will at first be thought hopeless to endeavor to carry similar plans into execution in other large cities, whether at home or in the United States. In reality, however, the sum bequeathed by Mr. Lowell for his foundation, though munificent, was by no means enormous, not much exceeding 70,000*l*., which, according to the usual fate awaiting donations for educational objects, would have been all swallowed up in the erection of costly buildings, after which the learned would be invited to share the scanty leavings of the 'Committee of Taste' and the merciless architect, —

'reliquias Danaum atque immitis Achillei.'

But in the present case the testator provided in his will that not a single dollar should be spent in brick and mortar, in consequence of which proviso a spacious room was at once hired, and the intentions of the donor carried immediately into effect, without a year's delay.

"If there be any who imagine that a donation might be so splendid as to render an anti-building clause superfluous, let them remember the history of the Girard bequest in Philadelphia. Half a million sterling, with the express desire of the testator that the expenditure on architectural ornament should be moderate! Yet this vast sum is so nearly consumed that it is doubtful whether the remaining funds will suffice for the completion of the palace, — splendid, indeed, but extremely ill-fitted for a school-house! It is evident that when a passion so strong as that for building is to be resisted, total abstinence alone, as in the case of spirituous liquors, will prove an adequate safeguard. In the 'old country,' the same fatal propensity has stood in the way of all the most spirited efforts of modern times to establish and endow new institutions for the diffusion of knowledge. It is well known that the sum expended on the purchase of the ground, and in the erection of that part of University College, London, the exterior of which is nearly complete, exceeded 100,000*l*., one third of which was spent on the portico and dome, or the purely ornamental, the rooms under the dome having remained useless, and not even fitted up at the expiration of fifteen years.

In the society of these honored names, the Lowells, the Lawrences, the Appletons, and the Jacksons, —

When the professor of chemistry inquired for the chimney of his laboratory, he was informed that there was none; and, to remove the defect, a flue was run up which encroached on a handsome staircase, and destroyed the symmetry of the architect's design. Still greater was the dismay of the anatomical professor on learning that his lecture-room was to conform to the classical model of an ancient theatre designed for the recitation of Greek plays. Sir Charles Bell remarked that an anatomical theatre, to be perfect, should approach as nearly as possible to the shape of a well, that every student might look down and see distinctly the subject under demonstration. At a considerable cost the room was altered so as to serve the ends for which it was wanted. The liberal sums contributed by the public for the foundation of a rival college were expended in like manner long before the academical body came into existence. When the professor of chemistry at King's College asked for his laboratory, he was told that it had been entirely forgotten in the plan, but that he might take the kitchen on the floor below, and by ingenious machinery carry up his apparatus for illustrating experiments, through a trap-door, into an upper story, where his lecture-room was placed.

"Still, these collegiate buildings, in support of which the public came forward so liberally, were left, like the Girard College, half finished; whereas, if the same funds had been devoted to the securing of teachers of high acquirements, station, character, and celebrity, and if rooms of moderate dimensions had been at first hired, while the classes of pupils remained small, a generation would not have been lost, the new institutions would have risen more rapidly to that high rank which they are one day destined to attain, and testamentary bequests would have flowed in more copiously for buildings well adapted to the known and ascertained wants of the establishment. None would then grudge the fluted column, the swelling dome, and the stately portico; and literature and science would continue to be the patrons of architecture, without being its victims.

"Prescott, in his admirable work on the Conquest of Mexico, remarks, when discussing the extent of the ancient Aztec civilization, that the progress made by the Mexicans in astronomy, and especially the fact of their having a general board of public education and the fine arts, proves more in favor of their advancement than the noble architectural monuments which they and their kindred tribes erected. 'Architecture,' he observes, 'is a sensual gratification, and addresses itself to the eye; it is the form in which the resources of a semi-civilized people are most likely to be lavished.'

"It has already appeared how admirably Mr. Lowell appreciated the exact point of semi-civilization which the Anglo-Saxon race had then attained on both sides of the Atlantic." — *Lyell's Travels.*

names with which he was familiar in his childhood, that he heard and lisped at the paternal fireside, that he met in his daily walks, in the public meeting, in the academic shade, in the social circle, in the marts of trade, and in the solemn assembly, — we leave the name of our departed friend; and in their communion and fellowship, among the spirits of just men made perfect in heaven, we leave the spirit of WILLIAM PARKINSON GREENE.

Alumni of the Free Academy, you have done your part towards perpetuating the memory of one of the most eminent of the founders of your *Alma Mater*. Having shared in the advantages resulting from his beneficence, you have resolved to transmit the remembrance of his virtues. The first recipients of his princely bounty and the witnesses of his daily life, you have determined, so far as your action can secure it, to pass down to those who shall come after you the moral legacy which he has left to this academic brotherhood and sisterhood. It is a filial, pious duty thus to enshrine the character of the man in whose fortune you have been permitted so generously to share. Let it be a matter of pride with you that the fortune and the character of your benefactor can blend so sweetly in your memories; that the former was the honest outgrowth of the latter. Let his bright example serve as a stimulus to your own lives. Remember the heroic virtue which impelled him early to choose a life of toil and usefulness instead of one of ease and pleasure. Inheriting a princely patrimony, which was largely increased by marriage, he might have passed a life of elegant leisure, secure from danger and fearless of reproach; he might have been content

> "To sport with Amaryllis in the shade,
> Or with the tangles of Neæra's hair;"

to live unknown and die unlamented. But the choice of Solomon was his; or rather, like the great Apostle, a necessity was laid upon him, a woe threatened him, if he did not devote life and fortune to the interests of his race and the service of his Maker. And when that fortune was scattered, he bated not a jot of heart or hope, but steered right onward to the accumulation of another; and, like the patriarch of Uz, whose character he so much admired, he received as the reward of his probity and enterprise greater wealth than he had at the beginning.

Be careful to remember that in his devotion to business he sacrificed not the higher elements of his character. The *man* was not lost in the *manufacturer*. Amid all the complications, anxieties, vexations, reverses, and successes of business, there was the steady culture and the luxuriant growth of the intellect and the heart. His intercourse with men brought him nearer to his God. His care for material interests only taught him the vast superiority of the moral and spiritual.

These are deeds and virtues which eminently befit the present period of your lives. It is true that he would have been the last to require or expect this service at your hands; and for that very reason it is the more incumbent on you to render it. He had fully conquered the last infirmity of noble minds. It was something more than a desire of vulgar fame, or fame of any kind, that raised his spirit

"To scorn delights and live laborious days."

Virtue with him was its own exceeding great reward.

Of the numberless throngs which our great English poet has brought to his temple of Fame as worshippers of the goddess and suppliants for her favors, he belongs in the smallest and the choicest class.

"Then came the smallest tribe I yet had seen;
Plain was their dress, and modest was their mien.
'Great idol of mankind! we neither claim
The praise of merit, nor aspire to fame.
'T is all we beg thee, to conceal from sight
Those acts of goodness which themselves requite.
Oh let us still the secret joy partake,
To follow virtue even for virtue's sake.'
"'And live there men who slight immortal Fame?
Who then with incense shall adore our name?
But, mortals! know, 't is still our greatest pride
To blaze those virtues which the good would hide.
Rise, Muses, rise! add all your tuneful breath;
These must not sleep in darkness and in death.'
She said: in air the trembling music floats,
And on the winds triumphant swell the notes;
So soft, though high, so loud, and yet so clear,
Even listening angels leaned from heaven to hear;
To farthest shores the ambrosial spirit flies,
Sweet to the world, and grateful to the skies."

APPENDIX.

NOTE A.

GARDINER GREENE, of Boston, was a descendant, in the fourth generation, of JOHN GREENE, who sailed from Southampton in April, 1635, in the ship "James," of London, William Cooper, master, and arrived at Boston on the 3d of June. He brought with him his wife and five children, — John, Peter, James, Thomas, and Mary. He removed to Rhode Island in the next company after Roger Williams, and was an associate with him in the Providence purchase of 1638. He became proprietor of a tract of land on Providence River, and south of the Pawtuxet, in 1642. He was also one of the original purchasers of Shawhomet, 1642-3. His wife died in 1643, in consequence of hardships suffered when Warwick (then Shawhomet) was attacked by a troop of horse. In 1644 he returned to England on business relative to Narragansett, and, while in England, married his second wife, Alice Daniels. He died at Warwick about 1659, and was buried at Conanicut.

His descendants occupy a most honorable place in Rhode Island history. In all the arts of peace and war they have rendered services to their State and country which will be recorded so long as Rhode Island or American history shall continue to be written. The founder of this noble *gens* was himself a magistrate, clerk of the council, and one of the principal inhabitants of the colony. He appears to have been an earnest and able associate with that great Christian statesman, the *protégé* of Sir Edward Coke, the relative, as some maintain, of Oliver Cromwell, and, as all agree, the intimate friend, the teacher, and the pupil of John Milton, who first enunciated distinctly to the world the true doctrine of soul-liberty, and made it the foundation of a Christian State; who was respected as a scholar in the halls of the English universities, as well as revered and beloved in the wigwams of Narragansett savages.

The farm on which John Greene was buried is still in the possession of one of his descendants of the same name.

The line of descent from John Greene is through THOMAS (born in England, 1631; died at Warwick, June 5, 1717); NATHANIEL (born April 10, 1679; removed to Boston; made his will August 6, and died August 8, 1714; mentions his land in Warwick given him by his father, Thomas Greene; also land which was granted to him near "Grinnage" [Greenwich?]); BENJAMIN (born at Boston, January 12, 1712; died 1776); to GARDINER GREENE, born September, 1753; died December 19, 1832.

GARDINER GREENE was thrice married.

1. ANN READING.

2. ELIZABETH HUBBARD, born March 23, 1760; married, November 28, 1788, in Boston; died September 7, 1797, in Boston. Their children were: *Mary Ann*, born April 19, 1790; married at Boston, June 8, 1815, to Samuel Hubbard; died July 10, 1827. They had five children. *Gardiner*, born January, 1792; died 1797. *Benjamin Daniel*, born at Demerara, December 29, 1793; married, 1826, Margaret M. Quincy; died October 14, 1862; no issue. *William Parkinson*, born September 7, 1795; married, July 14, 1819, Augusta Elizabeth Borland; died June 18, 1864. They had eight children.

3. ELIZABETH CLARKE COPLEY,* born in Boston, November 20, 1770; married, July 3, 1800, in London. Their chil-

---

* Miss Elizabeth Clarke Copley was the daughter of the great portrait and historical painter, John Singleton Copley, and sister of the celebrated Lord Lyndhurst. The family is remarkable for longevity, as well as talent. Lord Lyndhurst lived to the age of ninety, and his sister, Mrs. Greene, survives him at the age of ninety-five.

dren were: *Gardiner*, born April 21, 1802; died February 20, 1810. *Elizabeth Hubbard*, born March 20, 1804; died December 12, 1854. She married, December 27, 1826, Henry Timmins. They had five children. *Susanna*, born October 29, 1805; married, September 5, 1828, to Samuel Hammond; died March 22, 1844. They had two children. *Sarah*, born August 15, 1807; died at Paris, February 26, 1863. *John Singletan Copley*, born November 27, 1810; married, June 15, 1836, Elizabeth P. Hubbard. They had two children; no issue living. Married, November 5, 1844, Mary Ann Appleton. They had two children. Married, November 2, 1858, Belle W. McCulloch. They have two children. *Martha Babcock*, born November 15, 1812; married, October 15, 1832, Charles Amory. They had four children. *Mary Copley*, born July 17, 1817; married, August, 1837, to James Sullivan Amory. They had twelve children.

The residence of Mr. Gardiner Greene in Boston was on Tremont, near the head of Court Street. The site of his family mansion and grounds, which extended to Somerset Street, is now occupied by the rooms of the American Board of Commission for Foreign Missions, and Pemberton Square.

For most of the above facts I am indebted to the politeness of the Rev. J. S. C. Greene, of Brookline, Massachusetts. Further information of interest respecting John Greene may be gathered from Arnold's "History of the State of Rhode Island," Palfrey's "History of New England," Savage's "Genealogical Dictionary," and the lives of Roger Williams by James D. Knowles and William Gammell. See also "New England Historical and Genealogical Register," Vol. IV. p. 75.

NOTE B.

THE village of GREENEVILLE, now comprising a population of about three thousand souls, owes its existence to the various manufacturing operations which have arisen under the patronage of the NORWICH WATER-POWER COMPANY. This Company was chartered in 1829 under the following

ACT OF INCORPORATION.

At a General Assembly of the State of Connecticut, holden at Hartford, in said State, on the first Wednesday of May, in the year of our Lord one thousand eight hundred and twenty-nine;

Upon the memorial of James Lanman and others, of Norwich, in the county of New London, praying for an Act of Incorporation, as per memorial on file, dated May 2, 1829;

Resolved by this Assembly, That the said James Lanman, Calvin Goddard, George L. Perkins, William P. Greene, Henry Thomas, Joseph Perkins, William C. Gilman, Edward Whiting, Amos H. Hubbard, Russell Hubbard, Jedediah Huntington, Elisha H. Mansfield, John Lathrop, Erastus Coit, Cushing Eells, Dixwell Lathrop, Jr., Frank T. Lathrop, Erastus Davison, Arthur F. Gilman, James L. Ripley, Alpheus Kingsley, George O. Goodwin, Daniel L. Coit, Ralph Farnsworth, William D. Ripley, and Benjamin D. Greene, with all others who are, or shall hereafter become associated with them, be, and they hereby are, with their successors and assigns, made and established a body politic and corporate by the name of the NORWICH WATER-POWER COMPANY, for the purpose of purchasing and holding upon and near the Shetucket and Quinebaug Rivers, and preparing for use the water of said rivers, for manufacturing and other purposes, by the erection of dams and other necessary works, and of holding, letting, leasing, selling, and disposing of the use of such water-power in the most advantageous manner; and by that name they, and their successors and assigns, shall be, and hereby are authorized and empowered to purchase, take, hold, occupy, possess, and enjoy, to them and their successors, any goods, chattels, and effects of whatever kind they may be, the better to enable them to carry on such business to advantage; also, to purchase, take, hold, occupy, possess, and enjoy any such tenements, lands, hereditaments, in the towns of Norwich, Preston, and Lisbon, as shall be necessary for the views and purposes of said Company, and such other lands, tenements, hereditaments, as shall be taken in payment of, or as security for, debts due the said Company; and also to take a lease or leases of any such lands, tenements, or hereditaments, for a term of years, and the same to let, lease, sell, and dispose of, at pleasure ; also, to sue and be sued, plead and be impleaded, defend and be defended, answer and be answered unto, in any court of record, or elsewhere ; and said Company may have and use a common seal, and may alter the same at their pleasure.

Resolved, further, That the Capital Stock of said Company shall not exceed forty thousand dollars ; and that a share of said stock shall be five hundred dollars, and shall be deemed and considered personal estate, and be transferable only on the books of said Company, in such forms as the Directors of said Company may prescribe. And the said Company shall, at all times, have a lien upon all the stock or property of the members of said Company, invested therein, for all debts due from them to said Company ; and said Company may go into operation immediately.

Resolved, further, That the stock, property, and affairs of the said Company shall be managed by not less than five, nor more than seven, Directors, who shall hold their offices for one year ; which Directors shall be stockholders, and citizens of the United States, and a majority of them citizens of this State, and shall annually be elected at such time and place as the regulations of said Company shall prescribe. A majority of the Directors shall, on all occasions, when assembled according to the By-laws of the said Company, form a quorum for the transaction of business ; and the majority of stockholders present at any legal meeting shall be capable of transacting the business of that meeting, each share entitling the owner thereof to one vote ; and the first meeting of said Company shall be called by James Lanman, Calvin Goddard, and William P. Greene, or either two of them, by giving public notice thereof in one of the newspapers printed in the town of Norwich.

Resolved, further, That the Directors for the time being, or a major part of them, shall have power to fill any vacancy which may happen in their Board, by death, resignation, or otherwise, for the then current year ; and to appoint and employ, from time to time, a Secretary, Treasurer, and such other officers, mechanics, and laborers as they may think proper for the transaction of the business of the said Company ; and also to make and establish such By-laws, Rules, and Regulations as they shall think expedient for the better management of the concerns of said Company, and the same to alter and repeal, — *Pro-*

vided, always, That such By-laws, Rules, and Regulations shall not be inconsistent with the laws of this State or the United States; and such Directors may, at their discretion, from time to time, declare a dividend or dividends on each share, which shall be paid by the Treasurer of said Company.

Resolved, further, That if it shall so happen that an election of Directors shall not take place in any year at the annual meeting of the said Company, the Company, for that reason, shall not be dissolved; but such election may be held thereafter, on any convenient day within one year, to be fixed upon by the Directors, they previously giving public notice thereof.

Resolved, further, That the books of said Company containing their accounts shall, at all reasonable times, be open for the inspection of any of the stockholders of said Company; and as often as once in each year a statement of the accounts of said Company shall be made by order of the Directors.

Resolved, further, That the Directors may call in the subscriptions to the Capital Stock by instalments, in such proportions and at such times and places as they may think proper, giving notice thereof in a public newspaper printed at Norwich thirty days before the time of payment, and such other notice as the By-laws and Regulations of the said Company shall prescribe; and in case any stockholder shall neglect or refuse payment of such instalment or instalments, for the term of sixty days after the same shall become due and payable, and after he, she, or they have been notified thereof, such negligent stockholder or stockholders shall forfeit to said Company all his, her, or their previous instalments, together with all his, her, or their rights or interests whatever in said stock.

Resolved, further, That for the debts which may at any time be due from said Company, the stockholders shall not be responsible in their private capacity, but the property and estate of the said Company only.

Provided, That nothing contained in this act shall be construed to authorize or empower the said Company to use their funds for any banking transactions; *and also Provided*, That this grant shall be subject to be altered, amended, or repealed at the pleasure of the General Assembly.

Provided, further, That no dividend shall ever be made among the several stockholders, unless the remaining property of said Company shall be equal in value to at least twice the amount of debts then due from said Company.

A true copy of record, examined and certified under the seal of the State by THOMAS DAY,
Secretary.

At a General Assembly of the State of Connecticut, holden at New Haven, in said State, on the first Wednesday of May, in the year of our Lord one thousand eight hundred and thirty-two ;

Upon the petition of William P. Greene, in behalf of the Norwich Water-power Company, praying for an amendment of their charter so far as to authorize the increase of their Capital Stock from forty thousand to eighty thousand dollars as per petition on file ;

Resolved by this Assembly, That the said Company be, and they are hereby, authorized to increase the Capital Stock of said Company to an amount not exceeding the sum of eighty thousand dollars, and that said additional Capital Stock may be distributed in such manner as said Company shall direct.

A true copy of record, examined by THOMAS DAY,
Secretary.

Under the foregoing Act of Incorporation, operations were commenced upon the Shetucket in June, 1829. The work was under the direction of James F. Baldwin as chief, and W. T. Prentice as assistant engineer. Benjamin Durfey, the superintendent of labor, still lives to exercise, as the agent of the Water-power Company, a supervision of the work of which he saw the commencement. The dam and canal were completed in 1830, and the erection of mills for various branches of industry was begun in 1831. The following is believed to be a tolerably accurate list of the various enterprises which have from time to time sprung up on this foundation.

The first building on the canal was commenced in August, 1831. It was built by the Water-power Company for Noah Davis, and used by him for some years as a manufactory for bone buttons. Tweedy and Barrows carried on for a time the manufacture of German-silver in this building. It was burnt in May, 1837, and the foundations may still be seen near the waste weir.

The Greeneville Manufacturing Company, under the direction of William H. Coit and James L. Ripley, began in September, 1831, the erection of a mill for the manufacture of flannel, which, after being used for this purpose by the Greeneville Company for some time, passed into the hands of William F. Clark, who continued the same business for some years. From Mr. Clark the factory passed to the possession of Norton & Converse, and from them to Norton Brothers. During the present year, 1865, it has been partially burned, and has passed into the hands of Isaac Johnson, who carries on there the manufacture of wicking, twine, carpet yarns, and fine yarns.

In 1835, a wooden building was erected by the Water-power Company for Charles Spalding, which he occupied for some years as a paper-mill. William A. Buckingham manufactured carpet yarns here for a time. In 1858, Allen Cameron commenced here the manufacture of linen goods, and continued the business for about two years, when the building was again devoted to carpet yarns, until, in 1862, it was appropriated to the manufacture of shoddy goods by T. N. Dickenson, who now occupies it.

The Water-power Company in 1853 erected a brick building for the Greeneville Worsted Company, under the direction of Allen Cameron. Cameron was succeeded in 1858 by J. W. Dimick, and in 1861 the mill was purchased and enlarged by A. H. Hubbard & Company, who transferred their business from the Falls to Greeneville.

In 1839, a wooden grist-mill was built for Spalding & Alexander, (Jedediah Spalding and James D. Alexander,) which has passed through the hands of Abner C. Adams, N. T. Adams, James D. Mowry, and Robinson Northup, to the present proprietors, Samuel Mowry and Benjamin Durfey.

The Thames Company, in 1831–32, erected a large brick cotton-mill, the Quinebaug Mill, so called, which passed into the hands of the present proprietors, the Shetucket Company, in 1838, was burned May 26, 1842, rebuilt the following year, and has since been greatly enlarged.

In 1831, the Water-power Company built, for Kennedy & Tillinghast, a cotton-mill, which was occupied by them nearly twenty years. It was run for a year by Zebulon Whipple, and in 1853 passed into the hands of the present proprietor, Samuel Mowry, who uses it as a machine-shop and wooden-type manufactory.

In 1840, a bleachery was erected by the Water-power Company for Moses Pierce. It was burnt in November, 1859, immediately rebuilt, and is still occupied by Mr. Pierce.

In 1832, the Water-power Company built a paper-mill for David Smith, who organized the Chelsea Manufacturing Company. Mr. Smith eventually became the principal proprietor of the Company, but retired from the business in 1859. The Chelsea Company ceased to exist in 1865, and the mill is now run by Campbell, Hall & Company, of New York. This mill at one time was said to be the largest in the world.

A wooden building was erected in 1832 by the Water-power Company, which was occupied as a sash and blind factory by Hooker & Rice (J. W. Hooker and Edmund Rice). This was burned after a few years' occupancy, (May, 1837,) and was replaced by a paper-mill, which was conducted by Culver & Mickle. This mill also was burned, and has not been rebuilt. In the basement of this sash and blind factory, Oliver Allen manufactured woollen-machinery, and also commenced the manufacture of the "Bomb Lance," of which he was the inventor.

In 1850, William A. Buckingham erected the Dye Works, so called, where he carried on the business of dyeing for three years. In 1853, James Houston, who had superintended the business from the commencement, became proprietor, and still remains so.

The moral and religious wants of Greeneville were early subjects of attention with the proprietors of the village.

"William P. Greene, the originator of the Water-power Company, and his coadjutant, William C. Gilman," (I quote from the history of the Greeneville Congregational Church,) "were the prominent and efficient directors in all its movements. The moral and religious welfare of the community which was to be gathered upon their premises, were subjects of deep interest to them; and from the beginning this church and society have found them reliable friends and patrons. The Company neither furnished intoxicating liquors, nor allowed the use of them as a beverage on their works; and the conditions for the sale of their lands, with the rules for the conduct of all parties interested, are evidence of a wise forecast."

On the first of January, 1833, the GREENEVILLE CONGREGATIONAL CHURCH was constituted the Fourth Congregational Church of Norwich. The following is the succession of pastors: —

Rev. John Storrs, from March, 1834, to April, 1835.
" Spencer F. Beard supplied the pulpit for about two years.
" Stephen Crosby, 1837. Died June, 1838.
" A. L. Whitman, December, 1838, to March, 1846.
" C. P. Bush, December, 1846, to January, 1856.
" Robert P. Stanton, June, 1856, to the present time.

The meeting-house was begun in the autumn of 1834, and completed in the spring following, when it was dedicated by Dr. Hawes, of Hartford.

The GREENEVILLE BAPTIST CHURCH was constituted May 14, 1845.

Rev. D. B. Cheney was pastor from May 14, 1845, to May 5, 1847.
" Lawson Mussey, May 5, 1847, to Dec. 5, 1852.
" Niles Whiting, Dec. 5, 1852, to April 1, 1854.
" D. D. Lyon, April 1, 1854, to July 11, 1857.
" O. W. Gates, July 11, 1857, to Oct. 1, 1860.
" J. M. Phillips, Oct. 1, 1860, to Feb. 1, 1865.
" William W. Ashley, Feb. 1, 1865, the present pastor.

The first meeting-house was built in 1846, and was burnt in February, 1854. The present house of worship was erected the same year.

The first METHODIST house of worship was built in 1837. The present house was erected in 1864.

The CATHOLICS organized their first society in 1844. The services of the church (St. Mary's) for seven years were conducted by priests from the College of the Holy Cross, Worcester, Mass. In August, 1851, the Rev. Daniel Kelly assumed the care of the society, and still discharges the duties of the office. The first church was a small structure, only thirty-two feet by fifty; but it has been twice enlarged, and is now the most capacious in the city.

The interests of education received early attention from the founders and original inhabitants of this village. The entire village was first constituted into one school district, but was subsequently divided into two. These two were again united, and the schools were graded. The first principal teacher under the graded system was Mr. J. D. Giddings, a gentleman who deserves honorable mention as an educator. He taught, after leaving Greeneville, with great success as principal of one of the schools in Providence, R. I., was the first principal of the Hartford High School, and has the honor of being the first to establish the New-England system of free schools in Charleston, S. C. He was in Charleston during the entire period of the recent war, as many a prisoner can testify, from the relief which he experienced at his hands.

I regret that it is not in my power to give the succession of principal teachers from Mr. Giddings to the present time. I have been able to obtain their names only since 1856. They are as follows: —

Carlos C. Kimball, August, 1856, to March, 1857.
Nathan C. Pond, April, 1857, to April, 1859.
John F. Peck, April, 1859, to November, 1860.
Henry C. Davis, November, 1860, to July, 1862.

Joseph A. Kellogg, July, 1862, to July, 1863.
James L. Johnson, July, 1863, to April, 1865.
Amos F. Palmer, April, 1865, the present principal.

It is but justice to say that the Greeneville schools have for a series of years maintained a uniform character for excellence in all the elements that go to constitute thorough and successful education.

A good foundation for a village library was laid by William P. Greene some years since, in the hope that others would be interested in the enterprise, and carry it on; but it remains as yet where Mr. Greene left it.

NOTE C.

MANUFACTURING operations at Norwich Falls date from the first settlement of the town. It was here that John Elderkin erected his grist-mill at some time previous to November 1, 1661, if he fulfilled the terms of his contract of December 11, 1660, which is the first recorded act in the town books of Norwich. The site of Elderkin's mill, if tradition be correct, was below the Falls, at a point nearly opposite Sachem's Rock, the water being brought around the Falls by a trough or conduit. There are, however, perhaps, some reasons for believing that Elderkin may have built his mill above the Falls, in the neighborhood of the old paper-mill. It is at this point that we find the next mention of any manufacturing operations. In written documents of 1745, mention is made of "Bingham's mill," or "Huntington's mill," which, from the connection, makes it quite certain that a mill had been erected at a very early period in the history of the town, a short distance below the railroad bridge, and immediately under the rocky bluff where the old paper-mill now stands. There are still in existence a "lease" and "covenant," bearing date July 15, 1745, between Caleb Norman and Hezekiah Huntington, by which instruments Norman leases to Huntington, for the term of thirty-five years, "one acre of land more or less," in separate lots on both sides of the Yantic, above and below the present paper-mill bridge. In consideration of this lease from Norman, Huntington covenants with him to build a dam between the two above-mentioned parcels of land, and also across "the gutter or hollow that runs up to the ford-way over said river to Bingham's mill, otherwise called Huntington's mill, that stands on the said river." "And the said Caleb Norman, for himself, his heirs, executors, and administrators, doth hereby covenant, promise, and agree to and with the said Hezekiah Huntington, his heirs, executors, administrators, and assigns, to procure at his own cost and charge a ditch to be digged,* and the same to be kept open and in good repair at all times during the said term of thirty-five years, that shall be sufficient to receive and draw off the water that shall be drawn through the gates at the dam in the said gutter, sufficient for the use of the said mills, at least six feet and three inches below a level from the top of a rock lying at the southerly end of a ledge in the east side of the said gutter." The mills above referred to were a mill for the manufacture of linseed-oil, to be built by Huntington, and a fulling-mill, to be built by Norman. The dam referred to is the present dam immediately above the paper-mill bridge; after having stood one hundred and twenty years, being once rebuilt, and serving four generations of men, this dam of Huntington and Norman's (an humble work compared with more recent structures) will, the present year, cease from the service of man, and the place that now knows it will know it no more forever. Huntington built his oil-mill, as we learn by tradition, immediately below the present bridge. Of the fulling-mill of Norman I get no information. The oil-mill was subsequently removed further

---

* This ditch has now the appearance of a natural water-course, and forms thee asterly boundary of the island in the Yantic which separates the two bridges immediately below the dam of Huntington and Norman. The bridges were built in 1771. The removal of the old dam will, of course, tend to restore the natural connection between the island and the main land.

down the stream to the present site of Col. Converse's new brick mill.

The property passed, in 1770, from Hezekiah Huntington to Joshua Huntington, son-in-law of Hezekiah, and from his heirs in 1823, to the late Joseph H. Strong, who continued the manufacture of linseed-oil, and built, in 1822, a woollen-mill on the site of the present factory of the Bacon Manufacturing Company, which was burned in 1848, and replaced by the present structure in 1850. This new building was first occupied, in 1852, by Charles A. Converse for the manufacture of bits and augurs; and he continued this business there until 1863, when he turned his attention to the manufacture of arms in connection with the Bacon Manufacturing Company, who became lessees of a portion of the premises in 1859. This Company still continue the business. From Joseph H. Strong the property passed to his brother, the late Henry Strong, in 1839, and from his heirs to the present proprietor, Charles A. Converse, in 1853. During the war of 1812–15, John Sterry erected a small building, on the site now marked by what is termed the Silk-Dam, for the spinning of silk.* During the present year, Col. Converse is building a new stone dam, which will greatly increase the value of the property. In 1864, Col. Converse demolished the old oil-mill and grist-mill, and erected the present substantial and capacious building, in which he continues his grist-mill, but the greater portion of which is leased by J. Hunt Adams & Company for the cutting of corks by a machine which was devised by J. D. Crocker, of this city, and is believed to be by far the most effective of all that have been invented.

Above the dam of Huntington and Norman there existed, as has been mentioned, near the site of the present unoccupied paper-mill, a mill called Huntington's or Bingham's mill; but

---

* The manufacture of silk had received some attention in Norwich at quite an early period. Dr. Stiles, writing in 1792, speaks of having the year previous seen a pair of silk stockings which were spun and woven in Norwich.

I have been able to obtain no further information concerning it. At this point, in 1771, Christopher Leffingwell erected the first paper-mill in Connecticut. At subsequent periods, a fulling-mill, grist-mill, and chocolate-mill were carried on under the same roof with the paper-mill. In 1811, March 30, Russell Hubbard, Hezekiah F. Williams, and Thomas M. Huntington purchased of William Leffingwell, son of Christopher, the paper-mill property, with its appurtenances. In September, 1815, Thomas M. Huntington sold his share to Russell Hubbard, and in the same month and year, Joshua Huntington, as administrator of Hezekiah F. Williams's estate, sold to Hubbard the remaining share of the property. On becoming sole proprietor of the estate, Russell Hubbard sold one half to Dwight Ripley, who, for a little more than one year, was associated with Hubbard in the manufacture of paper. In December, 1816, Hubbard became sole proprietor, and so continued until 1837, when he formed a partnership with his brother, Amos H. Hubbard, which will receive our notice when we speak of the establishments below the Falls.

Passing now below the Falls, we find the first mills erected there to have been a grist-mill, saw-mill, and oil-mill, by Elijah Lathrop. In 1794, Andrew Huntington and Ebenezer Bushnell built a paper-mill on the site of the present stone building, until recently occupied by R. & A. H. Hubbard. The land was leased to them by Elijah Lathrop for the term of twenty years. Here they continued the manufacture of paper until May, 1818, when they sold the property to Amos Hallam Hubbard, who had already bought the land of John Lathrop, January 1, 1818, and who continued there in the same business until 1837, when the mill was burned. In the erection of the new mill, Amos H. Hubbard formed a partnership with his brother Russell, and the two mills above and below the Falls were carried on by this firm until the death of Russell Hubbard in June, 1857. Amos H. Hubbard continued the paper business here until the spring of 1861, when he disposed of the entire property to William P. Greene, as the representative of the Falls Company, for $55,000.

Nathaniel Howland and John G. Baxter leased, June 1, 1802, of Elijah and Simon Lathrop, for twenty years, the right to erect a building for the spinning and manufacturing of hemp, flax, wool, and cotton. This is generally known as the Duck Mill. Elijah and Simon Lathrop also leased to John Sterry and Epaphras Porter, May 27, 1806, the right for twenty years to erect a building and carry on the business of the "burnishing of paper," an art of which Sterry was the inventor.

In March, 1809, Elijah and Simon Lathrop conveyed these two leases, together with the rights and titles to the property, to Calvin Goddard, who, in connection with William Williams and William Williams, Jr., formed a company under the title of William Williams, Jr., & Company, who continued the corn and oil mills, and enlarged their works by the addition of a flour mill. In 1813, the Duck Mill, which had been built by Howland & Baxter, was converted into a cotton-mill by the last-mentioned Company, and then conducted by John Gray as their agent. In 1816, one of the corn-mills was converted into a nail factory, (Norwich Iron & Nail Company,) under the direction of William C. Gilman, who now for the first time appears as a manufacturer in Norwich. The nail business thus commenced was owned by four equal proprietors, namely, William C. Gilman, Lott & Seaman, Samuel T. Odiorne, and William Williams, Jr., & Company.

In 1819 the cotton-mill was reorganized under the title of the Williams Cotton Factory, with John De Witt as agent; and on his retirement, William C. Gilman became the agent, who was chiefly instrumental in first directing the attention of Boston capitalists to this city. In 1821, the entire property of the Williams Company was sold to Samuel Hubbard and others, of Boston, which led, in the year 1823, to the formation of

THE THAMES MANUFACTURING COMPANY.

This Company was incorporated by the legislature of Connecticut, as above stated, in May, 1823. By the politeness of Samuel Mowry, Esq., I have been favored with access to all the records of the stockholders and Directors from the commencement to the close of the concern. The first meeting of the stockholders, at which the act of incorporation was accepted, was held on the 18th of June, 1823. There were present at this meeting the following gentlemen, who were named in the charter as the first Board of Directors: Henry Hubbard, Benjamin D. Greene, William P. Greene, and William C. Gilman. John Hubbard and Samuel Hubbard appeared by attorney duly authorized. William P. Greene was appointed chairman *pro tempore*, and Arthur F. Gilman was appointed permanent clerk. At a meeting of the Directors on the 9th of July following, it was voted, —

That we carry into effect our original plan; that we erect a building, wheel, &c., for a cotton-mill of a capacity of two thousand spindles; that only one thousand spindles be put in in the first instance; that the amount of our capital be considered one hundred thousand dollars; that the amount of stock now subscribed being only seventy-five thousand dollars, the remaining twenty-five thousand be provided in one of the following modes : — 1st, by advances made by the several stockholders (excepting Henry Hubbard and William C. Gilman), in proportion to their original subscriptions; 2d, by creating new shares and procuring new associates; or 3d, by a loan taken up by the Company.

Voted, That a rolling and slitting mill be immediately erected.

Voted, That William P. Greene be associated with William C. Gilman, and that they be the agents of the Company; and that the erecting of the rolling and slitting mill be entirely committed to them, and also the general business of the Company.

On the 2d of March, 1824, it was voted that the agents erect a foundry, and carry the same immediately into operation, provided that the expense shall not exceed four thousand dollars. On the 29th of December, 1824, the agents were directed to purchase the Bozrah establishment, which was effected at an expense of twenty-two thousand five hundred dollars. In January, 1825, the Company voted to increase their capital stock to three hundred thousand dollars; and the first dividend of ten per cent. was declared in October of the same year.

The business of the Company appears to have been conducted satisfactorily to its stockholders for several years. At a meeting of the Directors in Boston, March 10, 1828, the following letter was received:—

To the President of the Thames Manufacturing Company:

Sir,—The object of my appointment as one of the agents of the Thames Company having been to exercise a general supervision in connection with their agent, William C. Gilman, during the erection of their works, and the same being now completed and in full operation, I would take the liberty through you of tendering to the Board of Directors the resignation of my office as one of their agents.

Very respectfully,
Your obedient servant,
WILLIAM P. GREENE.

NORWICH, *March 5*, 1828.

To this letter, the Directors, under date of April 8, 1828, returned the following reply:—

Willliam P. Greene, Esq., Norwich:

DEAR SIR,—The Directors of the Thames Manufacturing Company, in communicating to you their vote accepting your resignation as one of their agents, are desirous of expressing their views and feelings on the subject of your agency.

It had not been their wish or expectation that you should withdraw from the employment of the Company, and in consequence of it they recommitted the subject to you for your further deliberation and decision. On receiving your letter stating that you adhered to your first determination, they believed it to be their duty to act in immediate conformity to your wishes, and they accordingly accepted your resignation.

It is a pleasure to them to say that in the discharge of your agency you have given very great and very general satisfaction. The distinguished ability and integrity which have marked your conduct as an agent have been such as to entitle you to their warmest thanks, and they beg you to receive this communication as an expression of their approbation and confidence and friendship, and to be assured that the manner in which you have made known your intention to resign has added to the high respect they entertain for your character.

Though not entitled to your further services, the Directors hope they may from time to time receive your counsel and advice as the situation of the Company may seem to require it.

With their best wishes for your health and happiness, they are, in behalf of the Thames Manufacturing Company,

Your friends and servants,

SAMUEL HUBBARD,
JOHN D. WILLIAMS, } *Directors.*
JOHN BUMSTEAD,

It will be observed, by comparing dates, that by the resignation of his agency for the Thames Company more time was obtained by Mr. Greene for the enterprise on the Shetucket. It was accordingly in the following year that the Water-power Company was organized, and its operations commenced. This made way for the still further extension of the works of the Thames Company.

Immediately on the completion of the dam and canal on the Shetucket, the Thames Company turned their attention in this direction. After the subject had been carefully considered and reported on in previous meetings, it was voted unanimously at an adjournment of the annual meeting held on the 14th of September, 1831, —

That the Report of the committee [to whom the consideration of the subject had been referred] be accepted, and that the Directors, acting on the basis of the report, be hereby authorized, at their discretion, to purchase a site and erect a mill on the Shetucket, and to effect any loans which may be necessary for the purpose; but with the understanding that the Directors will make regular dividends whenever the profits will admit of it, notwithstanding the expenditure for the new mill.

At a meeting of the Directors on the following day, September 15, 1831, it was voted that William P. Greene, Mr. Gilman, and Mr. Mowry be a committee to mature plans for the building of machinery for the mill contemplated to be erected on the Shetucket, agreeably to the vote of the stockholders; and that the agent be authorized to carry said plans into effect with all convenient despatch after the mill privilege shall have been secured.

Voted, That Mr. Gilman be a committee to make a contract with the Norwich Water-power Company for a mill privilege of twelve thousand spindles, subject to the ratification of this Board.

The above votes of the Company and Board of Directors were carried into immediate effect.

The capital of the Company, now amounting to $400,000, was mainly invested in personal and real property, but a small portion being left free for conducting the regular operations of the Company. It will be observed that the new mill on the Shetucket was erected, not by an increase of the capital stock, but by a loan of $100,000 recommended and authorized, but never completely effected. The consequences of this undue extension soon began to be felt. In 1834 the condition of the Company's affairs was referred to a special committee, (Messrs. William Worthington and Henry Gassett,) whose report presents an elaborate and minute view of the situation of the Company, and recommends that the authorized loan of $100,000 be at once effected to remove the large floating debt, and free the agent from the embarrassments involved in its management. But the stockholders appear to have been unwilling to make further investments in this direction. The records of the Company and Board of Directors remind one of the remarks of the Hon. Nathan Appleton in his very timely pamphlet on the "Introduction of the Power-Loom and Origin of Lowell." "The chief trouble," he remarks, in speaking of the management of the Lowell companies at the same period, "is with those concerns which have attempted to get on with inadequate capital. The Lowell companies were all originally established on the principle that not more than two thirds of the capital should be invested in fixtures and machinery, leaving one third free to carry on the business. In some few instances this principle has been disadvantageously encroached upon, by increasing the original machinery without a proportionate increase of capital. One thing is certain, manufactures cannot be carried on to any great extent in this country in any other manner than by joint-stock companies. A large capital is necessary to success. Individuals possessing sufficient capital will not give themselves up to this pursuit. It is contrary to the genius of the country."

In the report of the same committee, Messrs. Worthington and Gassett, the following year, the same subject of an insufficient capital and the difficulties connected with a large floating debt was urged upon the attention of the stockholders, but with no better success. Quite a different course from that suggested was resolved on. At an adjourned annual meeting held in Boston, October 16, 1835, it was

Voted, That it is expedient to sell all the property of the Company except such as is connected with the establishment at the Quinebaug Mill [on the Shetucket].

In obedience to the preceding vote, the agent of the Company was instructed, at a meeting of the Directors held October 20, 1835, " to form plans and estimates, and endeavor to effect a sale of the Iron Works, the Thames Mill, and the Bozrah Mill, and with reference to finding associates in the city of New York." The prices fixed for the Thames and Bozrah mills were sixty-five and thirty-five thousand dollars respectively.

In order to perfect the sale of the Thames Mill, it became necessary to organize a new concern, under the name of the Norwich and New York Manufacturing Company. In doing this the agent retained an interest of ten thousand dollars for the Thames Company. From the first of January, 1836, the Thames Company may be regarded as having commenced a new state of business. The Thames Mill having been sold, the Bozrah and Quinebaug mills were set down at a reduced value. At the annual meeting, September 22, 1836, the affairs of the Company were referred to a new committee, consisting of William P. Greene, Edmund Monroe, and William C. Gilman. This committee submitted, through its chairman, the following

REPORT.

The Committee to whom was referred the present condition of the affairs of the Company, report:— That in their opinion its concerns cannot be conducted with any prospect of profitable results while the Company continues embarrassed with a large amount of debt; and unless some remedy be applied, in process of time the result will be the failure of the Company.

That if practicable to raise an additional capital of one hundred and fifty thousand dollars, effectual relief would be afforded; but the Company possess no power of raising this amount, either by assessment or by the sale of additional shares, and it cannot, therefore, be accomplished unless by the general agreement of the stockholders to take this amount in proportion to the shares now held by them respectively; and many of the stockholders are unwilling to make further advances. The only remaining alternatives which have accrued are, the sale of either a part or the whole of the property of the Company. That the sale of the Bozrah Mill, even if it were effected at the price heretofore authorized, would afford but partial relief; that the sale of the property on the Shetucket [the Quinebaug Mill] would leave comparatively so small an amount of property, that, if it were decided to sell that establishment, the stockholders would very generally prefer to sell the whole and close the concerns of the present Company; that it is very obvious that a sale cannot be effected unless on such terms as would present strong inducement to invest.

They therefore recommend that the concerns of the Thames Manufacturing Company shall be brought to a close as soon as the same can conveniently be done, and that the whole real estate of the Company shall be sold for the sum of one hundred thousand dollars, payable in three equal instalments at six, nine, and twelve months, with interest; that, to effect this object, a committee be appointed to form a company to make the purchase, with a capital of one hundred and sixty thousand dollars, to be divided into shares of one hundred dollars each; and that the stock in the said Company shall first be offered to the present proprietors, with the liberty of taking two shares for every share now owned by them respectively in the present Company, and the several parties to have until the first day of November to make their elections.

In compliance with the recommendations of this report, a

loan of one hundred thousand dollars from the stockholders to the Company was effected, mortgage upon the entire property being given as security. The relief expected from this measure, however, came too late. At a meeting of the Directors on the 17th of May, 1837, it was announced that the Company and their treasurer, Mr. Gilman, had suspended payment. The equity of redemption of the Company was sold on the 31st of August, 1837, to William C. Gilman.

The Thames Company having thus come to a close, the Quinebaug Mill passed into the hands of a new organization, the Shetucket Company, January 1, 1838, while the Norwich and New York Company, under the direction of Mr. Gilman, continued their business in the Thames Mill at the Falls for three or four years, when, on the failure of the Company, the property passed through the hands of the Quinebaug Bank and Edmund Smith, to the control of the present Falls Company, October, 1843, with Benjamin D. Greene, Samuel Mowry,* Denison B. Tucker, and William P. Greene as proprietors.

I should not forget to mention, that, in May, 1842, the Norwich and New York Company sold to Allen & Thurber (Ethan

---

* Samuel Mowry deserves honorable mention as one of the early and successful mechanics and manufacturers of Norwich. Mr. Mowry is a native of Killingly, was educated as a machinist, and built some of the first cotton machinery that was made in Connecticut. In 1821 he became connected with the cotton-mill at Bozrah, and in 1823 united his fortunes with the Thames Company, was one of the most active and able of its friends and at the close of its concerns received from its Directors the most honorable testimony to his ability and fidelity. He was one of the original proprietors in both the Falls and Shetucket Companies, and remained with them until 1853, when he established himself in his present position in the machine-shop at Greeneville. In connection with the general manufacture of machinery, he also carries on, with William H. Page, the manufacture of wooden type. At the age of threescore years and ten, he is reaping the reward of a life of industry and integrity, and is able to review the progress of manufacturing industry in this region from its commencement, and feel that he has borne an honorable part in bringing it to its present state of perfection and prosperity.

Allen and Charles Thurber) a lot immediately below, and contiguous to, the paper-mill of R. & A. H. Hubbard, for the purpose of building a pistol factory. This business was conducted on the basis of Ethan Allen's patent revolving six-barrel pistol, until July, 1847, when it was, under the direction of the same firm, removed to Worcester, Mass. Their factory at the Falls then passed into the hands of R. & A. H. Hubbard, and thence, April 1, 1861, to the Falls Company.

In reviewing the variety of manufacturing operations at the Falls, it is interesting to observe that the original business established there by Elderkin has held its ground through all the changes of two centuries. "King Cotton," even, has not been able as yet to dethrone his rival, "King Corn." Men now, as ever, are more solicitous for what they shall eat than for what they shall wear.

I have been able only to glance at some of the external facts connected with the industrial life of this community; and even these may appear to some as merely barren statistics, devoid of interest or instruction. That man, however, is little to be envied who can find neither interest nor instruction in tracing the successive steps by which a community advances in the acquisition of wealth, and in the mastery of all those arts which underlie our modern civilization. There is another class of facts, relating to what may be called the internal history of these manufactures, which I am obliged entirely to omit. Could "Goodman" Elderkin step into Col. Converse's grist-mill, he would hardly recognize it as the legitimate descendant of his primitive mechanism. But Elderkin, I imagine, would be quite as much at home in the grist-mill as would Howland & Baxter in the weaving-room of the present Falls Company. The Directors of the Thames Company, when they voted to erect a mill with a capacity for two thousand spindles, but with only one thousand at the commencement of operations, little thought that some of them would live to see more than seventeen thousand driven by the water-power then under their control. These comparisons remind us of the great improvements that have been made in machinery, and show us how quietly, and yet how rapidly, successive generations are devolving upon natural agents and mechanical combinations the toil that has engrossed the time and strength of mankind in past ages. The importance of recording all the facts relating to both the external and internal history of the mechanic arts is but partially recognized. There are those who find much to interest them in tracing the progress of the fashions, the different styles of dress, the mere shifting of the scenery that attends the march of generations across the stage of life, while the great forces and instrumentalities that are elevating each generation above its predecessor in material wealth and moral power are entirely disregarded.

The arts and the instruments of destruction, the marshalling of armies and navies, with all the cursed machinery of war, are far better understood than the blessed agencies and instrumentalities of peace that bear the race so gently onward and upward through the ages; just as the thunder-storm that shakes the firmament for an hour with its modicum of electric force, or the comet that flits across the heavens and startles the nations by its impalpable substance, is more regarded, and perhaps better understood, than the silent forces which urge revolving worlds through the infinite rounds of Neptune and Uranus, light up all the varied pageantry of earth and sky, the glorious pomp of day, the sparkling mysteries of night, and

> "Live through all life, extend through all extent,
> Spread undivided, operate unspent."

But the importance of these agencies and the utility of recording these facts are becoming better understood. The powers of production are beginning to be recognized as superior to the arts of destruction; and they have only commenced their beneficent career.

> "To martial arts shall milder arts succeed:
> Who blesses most shall gain the immortal meed."

I cannot close these brief notices of the manufactures of the Falls, without noticing the striking resemblance between their history and that of similar organizations in Massachusetts.

The men who originated these movements in the two States were neighbors and friends; the same difficulties were encountered, and the same reverses experienced. The first capital of the Waltham, or Boston Company was wholly expended before a yard of cloth had been made. But the Waltham mills have taught important lessons to the world, and Waltham cottons have been sold at a profit under the shadow of the European factories. The Boston Company was first in the field, and naturally formed the van in the great industrial march which has marked the century. But the Thames Company was not a tardy follower in the career of improvement. There appears to have existed between all these pioneer organizations an enlarged spirit of liberality, by which each was enabled to profit by any improvement of the others. Some of the machinery used at Norwich was manufactured at Waltham.* Waltham was the mother of Lowell, and gracefully yielded her best mechanic, Paul Moody, to the necessities of her aspiring daughter. We detect in such portions of the histories of these companies as have come to light scarcely a trace of that narrowness and exclusiveness which characterize the progress of similar arts in England.

Again, it should be observed that the organization of these companies was mainly due to family and kindred enterprise. Francis C. Lowell was brother-in-law of Patrick T. Jackson, and their "kith and kin" followed willingly their honorable and successful lead. The bare mention of the names of Appleton and Lawrence will suggest how important a part these families have acted in developing our manufacturing industry. The Thames Company was in a great measure a family enterprise, as the prominent names, during its whole history, will show. Samuel, John, and Henry Hubbard were the first purchasers of the property in Norwich which led to the formation of the Thames

---

* It is worthy of remark that Ebenezer Hobbs, M. D., who early became the agent of the Waltham Company, was a classmate and friend of Mr. Greene, and, like him, left the profession to which he had at first devoted himself, to engage in the rising interest of the manufacture of cotton.

Company. Samuel Hubbard, it has been seen, was the brother-in-law of Benjamin D. and William P. Greene. James Lloyd and John Borland, who were also stockholders in the Thames Company, were related by marriage to names already mentioned.

It is painful to hear, as we sometimes do, sweeping remarks affirming the oppression and grasping spirit of our great manufacturing proprietors. It is true their profits are sometimes large, but it is equally true that their losses are often disastrous. It is true that fortunes are sometimes made in a year, and it is no less true that they are often lost in an hour. Let any candid man, in moderate circumstances, follow carefully the history of many of our most prosperous manufacturing companies, and he will find much to make him satisfied with his lot. Let him consider the greatness of the original investment, the long time that must elapse before any profit is realized, the great variety of hazards to which this kind of property is exposed, the daily anxieties arising from all these hazards, and he will feel, if he feels rightly, that though there may be Shylocks engaged in the mechanic arts as well as in trade and finance, yet, as a class, manufacturers must be ranked very high as the benefactors of their generations.

The failure of the Thames Company, it will be observed, was a failure in form only, not in aim and achievement. The same names, the same objects, appear in the two companies that grew out of its ruins, as in the original organization. The manufacture of cotton at the Falls has not been a failure. The same gentleman who presided at the first meeting of the Thames stockholders, and bore his part so well in laying the foundations of a mill of two thousand spindles, lived to direct the movements of more than seventeen thousand on that very spot, and to render available a water-power of sixty thousand spindles in another portion of the city, and appropriating fourteen thousand to his own use.

In tracing the operations at the Falls and at Greeneville, I have frequently been tempted to mention facts that would present in a favorable light many interesting features of Mr. Greene's character. But this could hardly be done without reflecting upon the character or injuring the feelings of others. In no way could I do greater injustice to the memory of Mr. Greene than by recording any acts or achievements of his which would injure the honest fame of those who have gone with him to their final account, or produce an unpleasant sensation in any living bosom. There was no one feature of his character more interesting than his magnanimity towards those with whom he had come in collision in business transactions. I am the more inclined to this remark from the fact that I have heard it said that Mr. Greene was "vindictive" in his feelings towards those from whom he had occasion to differ in business relations. Nothing could be further from the truth; yet it is not difficult to understand how a casual observer should form such an opinion. Such was the strength of his character and the harmonious action of its elements, that, in opposing what he deemed a wrong course of action or a mistaken policy, he might appear to direct against the wrong-doer what was only meant for the wrong or the mischief which he was perpetrating. He might seem like an avenging angel when his heart was that of a child towards the fellow-man with whom he was engaged in controversy. He always seemed desirous to put the most charitable construction upon the motives and conduct of those with whom he came in collision. I have known him to go through weeks of anxious toil merely to be able to place a favorable construction upon conduct which had no other aspect than evil. If "to err is human, to forgive divine," it must be granted, that, while he claimed for himself no exemption from human frailty, he possessed in large measure that divine quality which in the Deity affords hope for our pardon. "Forgive us our trespasses *as we forgive those who trespass against us*" is a sentence that was often heard from his lips, and he would frequently direct attention to the concluding clause.

The METHODISTS were the first denomination to establish

religious worship at Norwich Falls. Their meeting-house on the Wharf Bridge, which was built in 1816, was carried away in 1823 by a flood. In the erection of a new church the attention of this denomination was directed to the rapidly increasing village at the Falls; and at this place, in 1825, their new house of worship was built and dedicated. This house continued to be used until 1853, when, on the dissolution of the Congregational church, the society purchased of Mr. Greene their present commodious edifice on Sachem Street. The former house is still standing on Lafayette Street, and is used as a carriage factory.

A CONGREGATIONAL church and society were organized in 1827, and a neat brick chapel erected the same year. This building is still standing, and is occupied as a storehouse by the Falls Company. Rev. Benson C. Baldwin was ordained as pastor, January 31, 1828. This connection was soon dissolved. The Rev. Charles Hyde was installed in 1830, and continued in the pastoral charge about three years. He was succeeded by Rev. J. W. Newton, who was ordained in 1834. Rev. Thomas J. Fessenden was the last pastor of this church. Its members at length united with the other Congregational churches in the city, and the house of worship, as above-mentioned, passed into the hands of the Methodists, in 1853.

The attention of the Thames Company was early turned to the importance of improving the means of education in the community that was springing up around their mills. The basement of the Congregational Chapel was fitted up for a school-room, and regular appropriations were made from time to time to promote the interests of education. The district system was continued until 1856, when the present tasteful and convenient building was erected to meet the increased wants of the population. In the erection of this house, Mr. Greene exhibited his usual foresight and generosity. As from two thirds to three quarters of the expense of the building would be paid by the Falls Company, the approbation of Mr. Greene was considered quite essential to the success of the undertaking. The plan submitted for his approval was for a much smaller school-house, to be built upon a very limited lot. Mr. Greene disapproved entirely of this plan, suggested an enlargement both of the house and lot, at an expense nearly double of what had been proposed, and then gave it his sanction.

In 1856-57 the present system of graded schools at the Falls was organized, under the direction of John N. Crandall, who remained the principal until the summer of 1857. He was succeeded by Arthur M. Wheeler, who occupied the post for one year. His successor was Benjamin B. Whittemore, who continued as principal until the spring of 1864, when he was succeeded by his brother, Nathaniel H. Whittemore, who resigned in the summer of 1865, and was succeeded by the present incumbent, Henry C. Davis, formerly principal of the Greeneville schools.

THE MANUFACTURE OF COTTON IN NORWICH.

To Norwich probably belongs the honor of being only the second town in New England to establish the manufacture of cotton. The honor of being the first is very generally accorded to Pawtucket. But Mr. Samuel Batchelder, in his recent valuable work on the "Introduction and Early Progress of the Cotton Manufacture in the United States," has shown that to Beverly, Massachusetts, and not to Pawtucket, Rhode Island, belongs the honor of establishing the first cotton factory in this country. The factory at Beverly was visited by Washington while on his tour through the New England States, in 1789, and its operations carefully noted. "In 1790," says Mr. Batchelder, in the work above mentioned, "a person who had been employed in the Beverly factory was engaged to go to Norwich, Connecticut, to put in operation some cotton machinery, which was understood to be similar to that used at Beverly. This machinery was not built in this country, but was supposed to have been imported by some means from England. The parties engaged in the business at Norwich were Mr. Huntington, Dr. Lathrop, and others." The cotton factory here referred to stood nearly opposite the present residence of Daniel L. Coit. No water was used, of course, but the motive power was derived from human hands. I have seen some of the products of this factory, and they do great credit to the skill of its operatives. Charles Bliss, Esq., has shown me specimens of cloth which were made here, and which were purchased in 1808 at sixty cents per yard. They are inferior in no respect to the best cotton fabrics of the present day. This factory, however, was not long continued. Its successor was the Duck Mill of Howland & Baxter; and this, as has been shown, was converted, in 1813, into a cotton-mill by William Williams, Jr., & Co. Then followed the Williams and Thames Companies. The Falls and Shetucket Companies now, I believe, monopolize the cotton manufacture within the limits of Norwich.

Falls Company. Capital, $500,000.
J. Baxter Upham, *President.*
James Lloyd Greene, *Secretary.*
Shetucket Company. Capital $500,000.
J. Baxter Upham, *President.*
James Lloyd Greene, *Secretary.*

The above companies represent in Norwich, at the present time, the results of the beginning in 1823. That beginning was based upon a capital of $75,000, which has now increased more than tenfold. One thousand spindles, in forty years, have been multiplied to more than thirty-one thousand; while an annual product too humble to mention in these days, has been augmented to more than ten millions of yards.*

* During the present year, 1865, foundations are laying for a vast increase in the industrial facilities of this city. The Occum Company, with a capital of $100,000, is constructing a dam in the northeasterly section of the town, which will afford water-power equal to that of Greeneville. Two cotton and one woollen mill are already in progress; and in the coming year another dam will doubtless be built, which will render available a still larger power. It is said by competent judges, that the amount of water-power in the vicinity of Norwich at present unemployed is equal to that of the whole of Rhode Island.

NOTE D.

The first charter for a railroad between Norwich and Boston was granted at the annual session of the general assembly of the State of Connecticut, in May, 1832, upon the petition of Jabez Huntington and others; and by its provisions William P. Greene, John Breed, William C. Gilman, Asa Child, and John A. Rockwell, their associates, successors, &c., were constituted a body politic and corporate, under the name of the "Boston, Norwich, and New London Railroad Company."

In March of the following year, 1833, the legislature of Massachusetts granted a charter, by the provisions of which Samuel Slater, Stephen Salisbury, and Jonathan Davis, their associates, successors, &c., were constituted a body politic and corporate, under the name of the "Worcester and Norwich Railroad Company."

By subsequent acts of the legislatures of Massachusetts and Connecticut, bearing date, respectively, April and May, 1836, the above-mentioned companies were united in one body corporate, under the name of the "Norwich and Worcester Railroad Company."

In the year 1837, the legislature of Massachusetts authorized the issue, upon certain conditions, of scrip or certificates of debt, in the name and behalf of the Commonwealth, for the sum of four hundred thousand dollars, to aid in the completion of the Norwich and Worcester Railroad. When application was made for the benefit of this act, a question arose as to whether the specified conditions had been complied with on the part of the Norwich and Worcester Railroad Company. The State authorities refused the issue of the scrip to the treasurer of the Company, and persisted in this refusal until Mr. Greene appeared before them and convinced them that the required conditions had been virtually and legally fulfilled.

By acts of the general assembly of Connecticut, passed in 1837 and 1839, the city of Norwich was authorized to issue certificates of debt to the amount of two hundred thousand dollars, in aid of the Norwich and Worcester Railroad Company. In the accomplishment of this object, so important to the success of the railroad, Mr. Greene bore a conspicuous and influential part.

NOTE E.

The following notices of Dr. Benjamin D. Greene are worthy of insertion here: —

"Benjamin Daniel Greene died in Boston, 14 October, 1862, aged 68 years. He was the eldest son of Gardiner and Elizabeth (Hubbard) Greene, and was born in Demerara, South America, — where his parents were then residing, — 22 December, 1793. His father was well known as the wealthiest citizen of Boston. His mother, whose virtues and amiable character were long remembered by her contemporaries, and who was a sister of the late John Hubbard, of Boston, died during his early childhood. Her maternal cares were assumed and fulfilled by Elizabeth Copley, a sister of Lord Lyndhurst, the present Mrs. Gardiner Greene, between whom and her adopted son a cordial affection subsisted through life. The subject of this notice was fitted for college in the Boston Latin School, where a Franklin medal was awarded him in 1807. He held a respectable rank in his class, and graduated with honors. After leaving college he became a student at law in Litchfield, Connecticut, and entered upon the practice of his profession, which he soon relinquished for that of medicine. Passing four years abroad, he travelled extensively in Europe, and completed his studies in the schools of Edinburgh and Paris. Attracted by scientific pursuits, he was highly appreciated as a botanist, and became the intimate friend and correspondent of Sir William Hooker, and other men of distinguished attainments. He was a liberal contributor to the Boston Society of Natural History; was its first President; and his valuable library, uncommonly rich in scientific works, was ever open to the researches of his associates. He was a member of the American Academy of Arts and Sciences.

"He married, 30 May, 1826, Margaret Morgan Quincy, daughter of Hon. Josiah Quincy, of Boston." — *Dr. Palmer's Necrology of Alumni of Harvard College.*

"At a meeting of the Boston Society of Natural History, 15 October, 1862, the President in the chair, Rev. Mr. Waterston announced the recent decease of Dr. B. D. Greene, of Boston, the first President of the Society. He spoke of the high personal character and scientific attainments of the deceased, and of the deep interest he ever felt in the welfare of the Society; in consideration of which, he moved that a committee of two be appointed to consider the best plan of procedure in reference to this loss. The President, Professor Agassiz, and Dr. Pickering followed, with remarks testifying to the great esteem in which Dr. Greene was universally held, and of his connection with the scientific world. Dr. Gould and Professor Rogers were appointed as the committee, to which were afterwards added the names of Professor Agassiz and Mr. Waterston.

"*November* 5, 1862. The committee appointed at the previous meeting to take suitable action with reference to the decease of Dr. B. D. Greene, being called upon, —

"Dr. A. A. Gould offered some preliminary statements with regard to Dr. Greene's connection with the early history of the Society, and then gave place to the introduction of resolutions by Professor W. B. Rogers.

"Professor W. B. Rogers said, that, before submitting to the Society the resolutions which he held in his hand, he was desirous of making a few remarks on the important services and peculiar virtues of our late valued friend and associate. He felt, indeed, that it was especially incumbent on him to offer in person a tribute of honor and gratitude to the memory of the deceased, as, on a former occasion, when called upon to address the Society in public, his imperfect knowledge of its early history had led him to overlook the distinguished part which Dr. Greene had taken in the formation and in the early nurture and guidance of the Society.

"It will be gratefully remembered by us all, that our associate, feeble as was his health at the time, united with us on that occasion in the celebration of our thirtieth anniversary. Who can doubt that a nature less noble than his would have seen, in the omission here referred to, a just cause for displeasure as well as surprise? But the large heart of our associate was too deeply interested in the good results of the zeal and liberality in which he had so earnestly shared to be much concerned about any apportionment of the honors so justly due to himself and the other founders and early friends of the Society. Soon after this occurrence, his usual kindly smile and cordial greeting gave touching proof that the much-regretted omission was as fully and freely forgiven as it had been unconsciously and innocently made.

"Without attempting a review of the scientific attainments and services of Dr. Greene, for which only the intimate and honored associates of his labors would be qualified, Professor Rogers begged simply to bring to the minds of the Society two points in the life and character of their late friend and associate, from which, as he thought, the wealthy and the learned here and everywhere might reap instruction.

"It is not often that the possessor of a liberal fortune is found giving his heart and time to the labor of scientific studies, which, however ennobling and replete with the purest of enjoyments, have, as we know, nothing in sympathy with the luxurious ease and brilliant excitements of what is called society. It is true, that, in the higher civilization to which the world is advancing, it may be confidently expected that the cultivation and promotion of knowledge and the nurture of all good enterprises will be recognized as the duty, and will become the noble aspiration, of all whose wealth offers them at once the leisure and the facility for such tastes and labors. Indeed, we already see among the most advanced communities bright auguries of this lofty social development; and in our city and State we may proudly point to many an example of affluence ennobled by large and profound culture, as well as by unstinted liberality in support of education and whatever else conduces to the happiness and progress of our race. Yet, it must be confessed that such tastes and labors as marked the life of our late colleague are still the exception, rather than the rule; and we are therefore especially called on to honor the memory of him who has furnished so beautiful and inspiring an example of them.

"But qualities still more rare than that here alluded to characterized the pursuits and conversation of our late colleague. No one could fail to remark his singular freedom from the ambitious impulses which, while they stimulate the labors of men of science, so often dim the clear beauty of their aspirations for what is true and beneficent. With him the love of knowledge, as gathered in the fields and in his precious library and herbarium, was a sufficing incentive and adequate reward. Delighting to store his mind with the beautiful truths gathered from the ample sources around him, and ever ready to help others devoting themselves to kindred branches of inquiry, and indeed to any scientific pursuits, his singular modesty shrunk from the least public exhibition of his various knowledge, and, in the eyes of those who knew his solid and diversified culture, gave to his social character its most peculiar and winning charm.

"Such were some of the services and characteristics of our late colleague, for which we owe him the tribute of our respect and reverence, and in testimony of which Professor Rogers concluded by submitting the following resolutions: —

"1. *Resolved*, That while it is the duty of the Society to hold in grateful recollection all who at any time may have participated in its labors or helped to enlarge its means of scientific usefulness, it is under especial obligations to honor the memory of the founders and early patrons of the Society, whose earnest zeal gave the first strong impulse to the pursuit of Natural History in this community, and whose liberal contributions and fostering care laid the foundation for those labors which have won for the Society an honorable place in the history of scientific investigation.

"2. *Resolved*, That the Society, while deeply regretting the loss which it has sustained in the death of its late associate, Dr. Benjamin

D. Greene, has a sad pleasure in placing on record an expression of its grateful and enduring reverence for his memory as one of the most zealous of its founders, as its first acting President, and as one of the most liberal of the patrons and co-workers of the Society.

"3. *Resolved*, That in expressing our sense of the great value of the services of our late associate to this Society, and of his worth as a cultivator and promoter of natural science, we would dwell with affectionate interest on the gentle graces of character for which he was remarkable, and especially on the shrinking modesty and reserve which veiled so beautifully the knowledge and culture they were unable to conceal.

"4. *Resolved*, That the Secretary be directed to transmit a copy of these resolutions to the family of the deceased.

"The resolutions were unanimously adopted."

The following notice of Dr. Greene was taken by the American Academy of Arts and Sciences, May 26, 1863: —

BENJAMIN D. GREENE, whom we have lost from our botanical section, died on the 14th of October last. He was born in Demerara, during the temporary sojourn of his parents there, in the year 1793, and was graduated at Harvard College in 1812. He first pursued legal studies, for a time in the then celebrated law-school at Litchfield, Connecticut, and was duly admitted to the bar in Boston. He then studied medicine, mainly in the schools of Paris and Scotland, and took the degree of M. D. at Edinburgh, in the year 1821. While pursuing these studies abroad, his scientific tastes were strongly developed, especially for botany, which, on his return home to the enjoyment of an ample fortune, now became the favorite pursuit of his life. His retiring, contemplative, and unambitious disposition rendered him averse to the toils, and wholly indifferent to the fame, of authorship. Of him it may especially be said, that he pursued his scientific studies for the pure gratification which they afforded him; but those who knew him are well aware that no small part of that gratification came from the pleasure which he took in freely placing his observations and his collections in the hands of those who could turn them to best account for the advancement of science. Perceiving that the great obstacles encountered by the naturalist here were the want of books and of authentic collections, he early and steadily endeavored to supply these desiderata, so far as he could, in one department, by gathering a choice botanical library, and a valuable herbarium, especially rich in authenticated specimens and in standard North American collections. These were most kindly placed at the disposal of working botanists, even those of distant parts of the country; and, to secure their continued usefulness, were at length, by gift and by bequest, consigned to the Boston Society of Natural History, — of which Mr. Greene was one of the founders, and the first President, — to which, besides, he bequeathed a large legacy in money.

In character, Mr. Greene was remarkably quiet and unobtrusive, yet highly sensible, cultivated, and discriminating. Eminently kind and disinterested, if he gave no thought to secure for himself a scientific reputation, he should all the more be remembered for the wise and considerate liberality through which he sought to promote the investigations of others in a chosen department of natural history.

NOTE F.

It is proper to record here the several objects to which the smaller contributions of Mr. Greene were applied.

Pianoforte (1857)	$354.00
Malby's Celestial and Terrestrial Globes (1857)	157.50
Portrait of Mr. Russell Hubbard, in part (1858)	200.00
Apparatus (1860)	600.00
Minerals (1862)	75.00
Contribution to salaries (1864)	250.00
Apparatus from the old Norwich Academy (estimated value)	83.25
	$1719.75

NOTE G.

At the bicentennial celebration of the settlement of Norwich, on the 7th and 8th of September, 1859, Gideon F. Thayer, of Boston, so well known as the founder of the Chauncy Hall School, and one of the leading men of his profession, in responding to a sentiment, made the following remarks in regard to the manner in which Mrs. Greene had seen fit to celebrate the birthday of her husband, and of the city of her adoption: —

"Sir, I am not a native of your beautiful city, nor connected with it by any of those ties or relations which give a claim to a part in this interesting celebration.

"About a year since, I attended a meeting of the American Institute of Instruction, held in this place. Arriving at ten o'clock in the evening, I could find no hotel accommodations, and accepted the kind offer of a friend to conduct me to private quarters, and repaired with him to the mansion of one of your principal citizens. My reception was cordial, and the hospitalities which I enjoyed were delicate, varied, and princely. These, and the attentions bestowed upon me elsewhere by others, almost made me a self-adopted son of Norwich; and, in some remarks which I was called on to make at the close of the session of the Institute, I stated that that was my first visit to your city, but it would not be the last by many a one.

"Through the whole succeeding year I was anticipating the pleasure of this celebration, and heartily rejoiced, as the time drew near, in the reception of an invitation to be present from my large-hearted host of 1858. I am now enjoying a repetition of last year's liberality and kindness, which time seems only to have increased and extended.

"Yesterday was not only the birthday of Norwich, but also that of my excellent host, whose estimable wife made a donation, valued at seven thousand dollars, to the Norwich Free Academy, and I had the satisfaction to write my name as a witness to their signatures to the noble deed of gift. It was, indeed, a real gratification to me; one that I should have deemed cheaply purchased at the cost of a journey from my home for it alone. This munificent donation, as you well know, consists of a dwelling-house and land for the use of the Principal of the Academy. How must every citizen of the place be inspired by the example, and incited to a zealous desire to support that which has been so nobly established."

FUNERAL AND COMMEMORATIVE SERVICES, RESOLUTIONS, &c.

At a meeting of the Alumni of the Norwich Free Academy, held in the Peck Library, the following preamble and resolutions were unanimously adopted: —

Whereas it has pleased Almighty God to take to himself the Hon. William P. Greene, late President of the Corporation and Board of Trustees of the Norwich Free Academy; therefore

Resolved, That, as Alumni of the Norwich Free Academy, we feel called to express our sense of the loss which we have sustained in the removal of one who was a principal founder and liberal patron of the institution in which we received our education.

Resolved, That we shall ever cherish a grateful remembrance of the manly and Christian virtues which adorned Mr. Greene's character, the early interest which he manifested in improving the schools of this city, his constant attention to all the higher interests of this community, and that it is to these labors of Mr. Greene, in connection with his large benevolence, we are greatly indebted for our own means of moral and intellectual improvement.

Resolved, That we deem it but a proper recognition of the virtues and services of Mr. Greene that some permanent record of his life should be made, which will inform those who shall come after us of the leading incidents of his life and the prominent features of his character.

Resolved, That we invite Mr. Elbridge Smith, the Principal of the Free Academy, to deliver before the Alumni, at such time as may suit his convenience, an Address commemorative of the life and character of our departed benefactor.

Resolved, That we tender to the family of Mr. Greene the assurance of our deepest sympathy in this their period of affliction.

Resolved, That copies of these resolutions, signed by the chairman and secretary of this meeting, be forwarded to the family of Mr. Greene.

NATHANIEL H. WHITTEMORE, *President.*

HENRY E. BOWERS, *Secretary.*

Services in commemoration of the late Hon. William P. Greene were held by the Alumni Association of the Norwich Free Academy on the evening of January 25th, 1865, in the following order: —

1. Hymn, by Miss L. A. W. Blackman.

>A house of mourning is this place,
>>Grief fills each heart to-day;
>For one we loved most tenderly
>>Has passed from earth away.
>
>This life is but one constant change, —
>>Friend meets with friend to part;
>The sundering of the closest ties
>>Must try each human heart.
>
>This honored servant of the Lord,
>>Whose heart was filled with love,
>Whose life was crowned with noble deeds,
>>Has gained his home above.
>
>His giant mind and manly heart,
>>Though linked with feeble clay,
>With youthful vigor, zeal, and power,
>>Bore the most perfect sway.
>
>This strength he gained from heavenly food,
>>While yet he lingered here;
>And thus his virtues brighter shone
>>With every passing year.

His love to God and all mankind,
  His charity so free,
His zeal to pave the way for youth
  To blest eternity, —

All find expression rare in these
  Our free and ample halls;
God bless his name, long may it shine,
  A sun within these walls.

2. Prayer, by the Rev. Hiram P. Arms, D. D.
3. Address, by Elbridge Smith, A. M.
4. Ode.

Not for him, but for us, should our tears now be shed:
Mourn, mourn for the living, but not for the dead;
Let the dirge be unsung, and awaken the psalm;
No cypress for him who lies crowned with the palm;
    Who has gone to his rest,
      When his labor was done,
    From the world he has blest,
      To the heaven he has won.

Though the light of his life to our vision is o'er,
The light of his spirit will burn evermore;
For truth in the world, like the sun in the skies,
Fades only to brighten, and sets but to rise.
    It moves ever onward,
      Though dimmed is its ray;
    And still on the earth
      It is day, — ever day.

How calmly he uttered his beautiful thought,
How meekly he bore all the honors it brought,
How bravely he spoke to oppression and wrong;
In that calmness, that meekness, that courage, how strong!
    Though with tears for his parting
      Our eyes may be dim,
    For ourselves they are falling,
      Not for him, — not for him.

We bless thee, O God, that the spirit is free
Which was true to itself, unto man, and to thee.
Thou hast called it from trial, released it from pain;
But its life and its teachings will ever remain.
  The good and the true
   Never die, — never die;
  Though gone, they are here,
   Ever nigh, — ever nigh.

At a meeting of the Trustees of the Norwich Free Academy, held at the house of Gen. William Williams on Saturday, June 18, 1864, the following preamble and resolutions were unanimously adopted: —

Whereas it has pleased our Heavenly Father to remove from this life the honored President of this Board, William Parkinson Greene, Esq.; therefore,

Resolved, That, in the opinion of this Board, the institution under its care has lost, by the death of Mr. Greene, one of the most enlightened of its original founders, one of its most liberal benefactors, a most efficient presiding officer, and one of its foremost and most judicious friends.

Resolved, That we record our most emphatic testimony to the great personal worth and distinguished ability of our departed President, his public spirit, his large benevolence, his warm and genial friendship, his firm integrity, his high moral courage, his ready appreciation and earnest grasp of every good enterprise, whether material, moral, or religious, his unfaltering devotion to whatever concerned the welfare of his fellow-men and the honor of his God.

Resolved, That we tender to his bereaved family the assurance of our warmest sympathy in this hour of their affliction.

Resolved, That, as a mark of our profound respect and affection for Mr. Greene, we will attend his funeral obsequies in a body, on Monday, the 20th instant.

Resolved, That the usual session of the Free Academy be suspended on the day of the funeral, and that the teachers and pupils be invited to unite with the Trustees in their last testimonial of respect to their departed friend.

Resolved, That the Secretary of this Board be directed to transmit a copy of these resolutions to the family of Mr. Greene, and that they be published in the "Norwich Daily Bulletin" and in the "Norwich Aurora."

WILLIAM WILLIAMS, *Chairman*.

ELBRIDGE SMITH, *Clerk*.

At a meeting of the Board of Directors of Thames Bank, held June 20, 1864, the following preamble and resolutions were passed:—

Having heard of the death of our friend, William P. Greene, the first President of this bank, we feel impelled by the grief which afflicts us to give it utterance in the only way in our power. From the establishment of this institution to the present time, in office and since he retired from it, Mr. Greene has been its firm friend, strong supporter, and ready helper. In our intercourse with him, in a business always large and sometimes perplexing, he has ever been open, candid, manly, and generous. He was to be depended on and correct. But as a friend, faithful, kind, cheerful, and affectionate, he made the deepest record on our hearts. We mourn our great loss; and therefore,

Resolved, That, as a Board of Directors, we will attend his funeral this afternoon, and direct that the Cashier send to the family of Mr. Greene a copy of this resolution, with our sympathy and respect, and publish the same in the city papers.

A true copy of record.

CHARLES BARD, *Cashier*.

The Common Council of the city of Norwich met at the council chamber on Saturday, June 18, 1864. Alderman Blackstone, in a few brief and touching remarks, announced the sudden death of the Hon. William P. Greene, and stated that the meeting was called for the purpose of taking such action relative thereto as might be deemed proper.

Councilman Whittemore also made a few brief remarks eulogistic of the deceased, whereupon the following preamble and resolutions were unanimously adopted:—

Whereas the sad intelligence has been communicated to this body of the sudden death of the Hon. William P. Greene, a former mayor of this city; be it therefore

Resolved, That, in the death of this distinguished citizen, who for nearly half a century has been connected with almost every enterprise calculated to promote the prosperity of the town and city of Norwich, this Board is called to mourn the loss of one whose noble and generous heart was ever ready to respond to the numerous calls from the poor and needy, to make liberal contributions in aid of the various beneficent and public institutions in our midst, and that we shall ever remember the manly virtues which have so endeared him to a large circle of friends and acquaintances.

Resolved, That as a token of respect for one whose strict integrity and purity of life were so conspicuous in his daily intercourse with all who were brought in contact with him, and to whom this city is so largely indebted for the many public improvements suggested by his comprehensive and sagacious mind, this Board will, as a body, attend his funeral on Monday next.

Resolved, That, as a further mark of respect to his memory, the city flag be displayed at half-mast during the day, and that our citizens be requested to close their places of business during the funeral ceremonies.

Resolved, That we tender to the relations of the deceased our profound sympathy in this afflicting dispensation of Divine Providence; and especially to our esteemed Mayor do we tender our heartfelt condolence in this bereavement, which has deprived him of a kind and affectionate father.

Resolved, That a copy of these resolutions be presented to the family of the deceased, attested by the Senior Alderman and Clerk.

LORENZO BLACKSTONE, *Senior Alderman.*
JOHN L. DEVOTION, *Clerk.*

THE attentive reader will notice some trifling discrepancies between the text of this Address and the Notes. These are due to the fact that in writing the text important information had not been received which was afterwards obtained.

An error occurs on page 21. The name of Mrs. Greene's father is stated to be Louis Vassail Borland; it should be Leonard Vassail Borland.

www.ingramcontent.com/pod-product-compliance
Lightning Source LLC
Chambersburg PA
CBHW030400170426
43202CB00010B/1434